# FRENCH PAINTING

# FRENCH PAINTING

## BASIL TAYLOR

12 COLOUR PLATES

AND 139 PHOTOGRAVURE PLATES

INTRODUCTORY NOTE BY

GEOFFREY GRIGSON

LONDON·THAMES AND HUDSON·NEW YORK

WE ARE INDEBTED TO DR. MARTIN HÜRLIMANN FOR THE
SELECTION OF PICTURES REPRODUCED IN THIS VOLUME

PRODUCED BY THAMES AND HUDSON LIMITED LONDON AND BY ATLANTIS VERLAG ZURICH
PRINTED IN GREAT BRITAIN BY JARROLD AND SONS LIMITED NORWICH 1951
COLOUR AND GRAVURE PLATES PRINTED BY ETABLISSEMENTS BRAUN AND CIE MULHOUSE

# INTRODUCTORY NOTE

WHAT is the essence of French painting? We should not ask this question, difficult, perhaps pointless, and impossible to answer, unless we were all agreed now
about the pre-eminence of this French painting for a long, long while. Not so old an
agreement. No Englishman, no German, no Italian, to choose from the near neighbours of
the French in the Old World, would at one time have thought so much of French art as
we do. The idea that, as once in Italy, this particular art was being kept alive for the Western
peoples in France, would have been to them ridiculous.

Take some English views in 1824, 1855, and 1911. When his pictures were stirring Paris
in 1824, Constable wrote savagely of the lack of "nature" in French art. Laboriously the
French artist studied art and nothing else. French painters knew as much of nature as a London
coach horse of a meadow. "In fact they do worse," said Constable as if he had been
a Frenchman of 1855 criticising the English pre-Raphaelites, "they make painful studies of
individual articles—leaves, rocks, stones, trees, etc., singly, so that they look cut out, without
belonging to the whole, and they neglect the look of nature altogether." At another time he
recoiled from the pictures of David, who seemed to Constable "to have formed his mind on
three sources—the *Scaffold*, the *hospital*, and a *bawdy house*".

An intelligent painter and critic went from London to the Paris exhibition of 1855. He
examined Courbet's *L'Atelier*, and was outraged. The whole work was wrought "with the
execution of a house-painter who has just taken up art. . . . Truly this is a strange people!
Side by side with this work, a picture of our Lord's Agony or of the Blessed Virgin will
probably be hung."

When the Post-Impressionists were exhibited in London forty-one years ago, another
Englishman who was both painter and critic, and no fool, looked at Cézanne and condemned
his "persistent personal clumsiness of touch". He was an artist of "modest rank" and no great
intellectual power. But he was "honest", his landscapes were "sincere" and had—at times—a
"real force". It is a good rule never to make fun of your grandparents, because to your grand-
children many of your own reactions will appear as fantastic. And these opinions of
1824, 1855, and 1910 were not rankly provincial nor were they mere acts of service to
the time; they had their parallels everywhere. In those years French painting was still
in progress, movement was succeeding movement in what we now see was the capital of the
graphic arts.

I am not sure that the impetus of French painting has not died away at last in a blaze of
disintegration. A phase of magnificent art rooted distantly in the European culture of the

Middle Ages has perhaps come to an end. The gallery has filled; and since we can look back through the achievements, we can now say with unanimity, Englishman, German, Italian, American, how great! how wonderful! Before all the pictures get too stale (as they may, after another fifty years) we should take our opportunity, and fill ourselves with the pleasure they can give.

Some of the causes of the greatness of French art, some indications of the essence, were revealed in those English condemnations. Put them the other way round, as virtues. The French painters, said Constable, were very laborious students of art. They had been, they were, they continued to be. David formed his style from the scaffold, the hospital and the bawdy house, and—thirty-one years later—this strange people, the French, can put alongside a nativity or a crucifixion a "coarse" painting of an artist in his studio with a naked model. Exactly. Nature (since Constable was not altogether contradicting himself) is not only the nature of leaves, skies and light; and these strange painters whom Constable taught again to look at *his* nature, also looked at the rest of nature, good and bad. Bethlehem and Golgotha are complementary, you must see, you must understand, both or neither; and supposing Constable had been right about David, there is after all an illuminating power in the study of the scaffold and the bawdy house. Constable could have read his New Testament with more attention. There were two Marys and there was Calvary.

Cézanne was honest, though "clumsy"; honesty among other qualities gave that real force to his landscape. Honesty. Just so. These strange *inclusive* artists, taking one with another, were honest so frequently, were so forceful, that force and honesty were bequeathed by them as elements in the French tradition. Honest and forceful poets in England in the same way made possible through the centuries a tradition of great poetry. Overawed by French art from Poussin or as far back as this book goes, we have at later times fawned upon Paris or France. But not everyone is strong in a national succession of painters. The weak in France as elsewhere needed fortifying; and nothing is more exhilarating than to see how the more vital French artists have helped the less vital ones into competence—for example, to see how the sane splendour of Poussin (for ever, after his time, in the germ-cells of French painting) raises Le Brun, Bourdon or Le Sueur, how the irrefutable truth of Watteau's drawing strengthens the hesitating draughtsmanship of Lancret or Boucher, or how the underrated severities of David checked a finical trickiness in Ingres's overrated line; and what health and what force were handed on by Courbet and by Cézanne!

Delacroix said once that his English friend Bonington was swept away by his mere skill; he had a coquettish touch, sacrificing good qualities "to an unhappy facility". In France enough men of genius have gone their own way, improving and not sacrificing their qualities, preserving, as Degas said the artist must do, their "innocence of personality", making art a profession and not a game, eschewing the carriage-and-pair, and so maintaining at fifty the genius of twenty-five.

"I am going on with my researches," wrote Cézanne not long before his death, ". . . I am continually making observations from nature, and I feel that I am making some slight progress . . . but I am old, ill, and I have sworn to die painting rather than to sink into the nasty corruption that threatens old men who allow themselves to be dominated by degrading passions." There is heroism in the tradition of art as much as in the tradition of navies. But tradition is what you need for the efflorescence of any school. The accident of genetics probably provides as many potential artists in one population as another. But if there is no tradition of painting the seed has come into stony ground.

Does it matter if there is or is not some tincture of France about the work of her painters, supposing that you could isolate it in every picture from the Middle Ages to Matisse? I think not. The parachute drops you, ignorant of your whereabouts, into one of the territories of art. You may recognise by the shape of the telegraph insulators, by railway crossings, by fields, faces, clothes, the country you are in. But these are qualities or tinctures of the surface. The qualities which matter are universal, not local or national.

"The finest virtues of French painting" Mr. Basil Taylor describes as "that French gift for assimilating creatively the influences of other artists and other schools, the power to exercise reason with passion." In other words, the finest French virtues are one each of the finest *human* gifts and *human* powers. Much varied good painting by the French (there is plenty of the ridiculous journalism of art in France as everywhere else) is neither handcuffed nor on the loose. Less than in other countries has the Frenchman mistaken one element for the elements combined or allowed a few cells to break away in a cancerous rebellion and masquerade as the organism of a work of art; which means that the essence of French painting has been—painting itself.

I do not inside me much care for the history of art. I observe its professors, I realise it may yet kill the effect of art upon our living. Nor do I believe in the immortality of the good work, which can at last become ineffective and alien and should then be allowed to die. But picture books I believe in, when they are not too miscellaneous. They introduce meanwhile such living pictures as there are, they help us to find these pictures, if we can, and so to enter their field of magnetism; and afterwards they are reminders of them.

"There are no schools; there are only painters." The art historian can prove absolutely that Courbet was talking nonsense, but let us have also the nonsense of the wise. Perhaps Courbet did not say enough. There are no schools, there are no painters, there are only pictures. And these, either dead or alive.

GEOFFREY GRIGSON

DELACROIX wrote in his journal that David's paintings were "a strange mixture of realism and idealism". However strange that particular synthesis may have appeared, it is one common in French art, in whatever sense one interprets the word idealism. Geographically, France is set between the North and the South, with one frontier against the Mediterranean and another against the Low Countries. For the five centuries of this book, the influence of Italy or the Netherlands, of Raphael or Rubens, their predecessors and successors, flowed across these frontiers or was sought by French artists. The seventeenth-century clash between the *Rubénistes* and the *Poussinistes* was a recurrent and not a temporary theme in the history of French art and French taste. Fouquet, Poussin, Claude, Watteau, Chardin, David, Ingres, Géricault, Delacroix, Courbet, Renoir, Cézanne, Seurat, in all these artists the synthesis of realism and idealism is there, the influence of North or South creatively transformed into something original and unmistakably French.

The beginnings of French painting are closely linked with the Early Renaissance painters of Italy, largely due to the removal of the Popes from Rome to Avignon soon after the start of the fourteenth century. It is appropriate, therefore, that the first illustration in this book should reproduce a part of those much-damaged, much-restored frescoes in the Garderobe Tower of the Palais des Papes at Avignon, for although the earliest easel pictures in the history of French painting come from Paris, it was the ancient southern province of Provence in which the patronage of the arts had existed longer than anywhere else in France. Again by the beginning of the fifteenth century, Paris had lost to other regional centres its place as the heart of the country's artistic life.

The Popes who had occupied the Palace at Avignon between 1305 and 1378 had commissioned artists from Italy, mainly from Siena, to decorate its walls with religious frescoes. Simone Martini was one of those Sienese masters attracted to Provence, and he died there five years after his arrival in 1339.

The paintings in this small room in the Garderobe Tower are, however, by French painters. They show scenes of courtly life, of hawking and fishing, bathing and fruit gathering. With their dense pattern of grasses, plants and leafage, their slim rhythmical figures and their evidence of the painters' delight in recording the details of nature, they closely resemble the tapestries not only of that period, but, indeed, such later masterpieces as *La Dame à la Licorne*. They must also be similar to the lost frescoes which Charles V commissioned for the old Louvre and for his queen's palace at Sol. The mood of this room is a reminder of the profane innocence of Watteau's *Fêtes,* and the leafy groves which form the setting are as oppressive in their pattern as the invented jungles of the Douanier Rosseau.

The cosmopolitan tendencies of the Avignon school continued after the papal patronage had ceased, and the paintings of *Le Bienheureux Pierre de Luxembourg presenting a Donor to the Virgin* and of *The Virgin presenting a Cistercian Monk to the 'Christ de Pitié'* (Plates 2 and 4) both clearly show the continuance of the Sienese influence into the fifteenth century. Here are the flat, decorative silhouettes, the relaxed, flowing contours and the schematic draperies which are the marks of Sienese art. This saint—Bienheureux Pierre de Luxembourg—who was made Cardinal at the age of fifteen and died three years later—was particularly venerated in Avignon where he was buried. The second image of him (Plate 3) retains the archaic decorative flatness, but the drapery has acquired the greater breadth and realism of a later time.

For thirty years after 1410 the school of Avignon suffered a decline, but the middle of the century brought with it three of the masterpieces of the age, Enguerrand de Charonton's *Coronation of the Virgin* (Plate 11), the anonymous *Pietà de Villeneuve* (Plate 29) and the *Retable de Boulbon*.

Enguerrand de Charonton was born in the diocese of Laon about 1410 and worked in Avignon between 1447 and 1461. The *Coronation of the Virgin* is a curious combination of mediæval imagery and design with the observation appropriate to the painter's own time. He has followed with minute exactitude the details laid down in the commission of his patron, Jean de Mostagnac. The panel is divided into various zones, and in each of these the scale of the figures varies. In Heaven the Virgin is being crowned by the Holy Trinity, while to the right and left the Beatific Vision is represented on a smaller scale, with figures of angels, saints, beatified souls and people of every class and rank. Below this again is the Earth, with the city of Rome, the Mass of St. Gregory, the Crucifixus and the Burning Bush, while at the lowest level is Purgatory and Hell inhabited by a crowd of tiny figures. The pattern is similar to that followed in the tympana of such cathedrals as Vézelay or Chartres, and the figures in Heaven and Paradise have been assembled in strict and hieratic order, stiff in their gestures and with fixed expressions. Hell and Purgatory, on the other hand, are painted with something like an impressionist vivacity, and apart from the natural, lively gestures of the little figures, many features of the Provençal landscape are clearly recognisable, including Mont St. Victoire. This painter's other identifiable work is the *Virgin of Mercy* (Plate 12) completed two years before, in 1452.

Throughout the works of the Avignon school there is a note of austerity and even disillusion. The *Pietà de Villeneuve* is not only the finest creation of the school, but one of the great tragic utterances of European painting. The wretched condition in which the panel has come down to us hardly diminishes its effect, for whatever individual detail may have been lost, it is through the contours and movements of the four central figures and in particular the agonising pattern of the dead Christ that the picture's message is communicated. There has seldom been a more subtle piece of pictorial architecture than this, in which the bent back of the Magdalen takes up the curves of the lifeless body, this mounting rhythm being then tempered by the more restrained movement of the Virgin. Above all there is the powerful image of Christ's right arm and of that tense rectangular shape which seems both to assault the body with its sharp corner and at the same time to bear it towards some unpredictable resurrection. In the Académie Royale in the seventeenth century, much time was to be devoted to discussing current theories of expression and significant gesture. No pictorial devices of that period were nearly so powerful as the imperceptible gestures of these mourners and their remote, introverted grief. The figure of the Donor is one of the greatest of French portraits, and for once he is no intruder upon the mood of the subject. Confronted by such a masterpiece we have reason to think that the advance of spatial realism did much to destroy the painter's command of tragedy, and it is significant that in some of the most moving expressions of grief in the art of the Renaissance and the Baroque, when any competent painter could give the illusion of distance, space is either restricted or unexplained. Botticelli's *Pietà* at Munich, Titian's *Pietà* in the Prado and El Greco's *Burial of Count Orgaz* are three notable examples.

Jean Fouquet's *Pietà* at Nouans (Plate 18) is much closer to Renaissance habits of picture making than the Avignon picture, but its more complicated pattern of solid forms in space diffuses the subject's meaning. In the Villeneuve *Pietà* the bare silhouette of domes and hills is sufficient to establish symbolically the emptiness of the world.

Two other pictures from Southern France, Louis Bréa's Altarpiece of the *Pietà with Sts. Martin and Catherine* (Plates 20 and 21) and the anonymous *Adoration of the Child* from Avignon (Plate 30), show the weakening of the school's expressiveness under growing foreign—particularly Italian—influences, though the portrait of the *Donor* (Plate 31) in the latter picture does reveal a tender realism which is akin to the Master of Moulins, though without the refinement of that painter's observation.

Besides Avignon, Aix was an important centre of the arts in the fifteenth century. There, in the church of La Madeleine, is the central panel of *The Annunciation* (Plate 6) from a triptych by that unknown painter who has been called the Master of the Annunciation of Aix. The side panels have been scattered among other collections. This work has caused much controversy among scholars who have found in it traces of Flemish or Burgundian or Italian authorship. The resemblances, in detail, to Flemish painting are certainly very marked; especially to the art of Jan van Eyck who, ten years before the likely date of this triptych, 1445, had painted his Altarpiece of the Lamb for Philippe le Bon, Duke of Burgundy and in about 1433 had completed his *Virgin with Chancellor Rollin* for the church of Notre Dame at Autun. The piles of books and papers which the painter has set above the figures of the prophets in the side panels (Plates 5 and 9) are among the earliest still lifes in European art; while they are just what a Flemish artist might have contrived to fill such a space, they have the selective realism of a still life by Chardin (Plates 83 and 83a).

It has recently been suggested that the Master of the Annunciation of Aix may indeed have been one of those artists attached to the court of King René of Anjou, brother-in-law of Charles VII. René, himself an artist, a painter and a writer, was related to the poet Charles d'Orléans. He was one of the strangest personalities of the century. In the course of those political adventures which gained and lost him so much territory and so many fortunes, he came to know the cultures of Western Europe, of the Netherlands, of Burgundy and the Mediterranean, with an intimacy shared by very few of his contemporaries. He employed at least two Italian artists, and among his counsellors were scholars with a deep knowledge of Italian. He may well have instructed in the new resources of Italian painting the French artists who surrounded him, and he is supposed to have given to Colantonio, Antonello da Messina's master, his knowledge of Flemish techniques.

Among those who worked for this cosmopolitan count of Anjou were the mysterious Maître des Heures de Rohan whose violent, expressionist pictures are among the most powerful statements of that tortured unrest of the years after Agincourt, and the René Master whose poetic compositions illustrating his patron's chivalrous romances would surely have appealed to the Pre-Raphaelites, had they known his work.

Another work in Aix Cathedral, Nicholas Froment's *Moses and the Burning Bush* (Plate 19) was, as contemporary documents prove, commissioned by René. He appears in the left-hand panel of the triptych, and his second wife, Jean Laval, in the other. This work was completed in 1476. The substitution of the Madonna for the image of God the Father among the burning branches retains the mediæval conception of the indestructible bush as a symbol of the woman who preserved her virginity after motherhood. The picture aspires to be modern, to combine a wholely symbolic imagery with a real world of space and physical presences. Yet,

11

how awkward and provincial it appears beside the best of the Italian Quattrocento or, indeed, beside the best which that century could produce in France, from the formalism of the Villeneuve *Pietà* to the realism of the Master of Moulins! For all the careful calculations in the landscape, the diminishing coils of the river and the chain of trees which punctuates its course, the composition is cramped, not spacious. The figures find difficulty in accommodating themselves within the frame and are not in harmony with their surroundings. There are hints of Italian influence; Moses, with his great protruding foot, has a Flemish angularity and Flemish features. Whereas *The Annunciation* of Aix suggests a happy synthesis of Northern and Southern knowledge and sensibility, this picture suffers from an unconvincing eclecticism and has not even that harsh naïvety which is an attractive feature of Froment's Lazarus triptych in the Uffizi. Is René to blame, perhaps, for a rash ambition to work beyond his resources?

*

THE OTHER predominant school of painting flourished in the region of the Loire, with the city of Tours as its centre, and it was there, in about 1420, that the greatest artist of the century, Jean Fouquet, was born. His youth and early years as a painter coincided with the period of despondency caused by the French defeat at the battle of Agincourt in 1415; his most produc-tive phase was to accompany that remarkable rebirth which followed the ultimate departure of the English armies. After Agincourt, the ensuing peace of Troyes, and the death of his father in 1422, the Dauphin Charles rejected all idea of becoming king and retired to his castle of Bourges. But the inspiration of Joan of Arc gave the French the faith and the leader-ship that they had temporarily lost: by 1435, four years after her execution, the costly and destructive civil wars had ended, and within another year the Dauphin had been crowned in Paris as Charles VII. By 1453 the English had been turned out of every corner of France except Calais and the Channel Islands. These years had also seen the reconstruction of the country's economy and a succession of measures to restore the monarchy's power against lawlessness and insecurity.

Fouquet came to Paris from Tours about 1440 and there learned his art in contact with what had survived of the old Paris school of miniature painting and, no doubt, with the new realism of such Flemish masters as Jan van Eyck and Roger van der Weyden. Between 1445 and 1447 he was in Rome, where he painted a portrait on panel of Pope Eugene IV. There he is likely to have seen works which were the foundation and support of Italian painting for two centuries: the frescoes by Masaccio and Masolino in the churches of San Clemente and Santa Maria Maggiore. Fra Angelico was at that time working in Santa Maria Sopra Minerva and the Chapel of the Sacraments in the Vatican. Furthermore, Fouquet could have studied Alberti's treatise *Della Pittura*, Ghiberti's *Commentarii* and may indeed have come into touch with the paintings or the writing of Piero della Francesca.

It was soon after his return from Italy to Tours, where he remained and opened his work-shop, that he painted the Melun Diptych (Plates 15–17) for Étienne Chevalier, who appears with St. Stephen in the left-hand panel. Chevalier had been Ambassador to England, was then *Trésorier* and was to become Charles' Secretary of State. It was during the next ten years that Fouquet's finest surviving works were painted, the miniature illustrations for the Book of Hours of Étienne Chevalier, for Boccaccio and for the *Grandes Chroniques de France*; the portraits of Charles and his chancellor, Guillaume Juvenal des Ursins. When Charles VII died in 1461, Fouquet designed the decorations for Louis XI's entry into Paris; he kept his position under the new king, being appointed 'Peintre du Roy' in 1474. Two years later when the King of Portugal visited Louis at Tours, he was commissioned to design the painted canopy used in the ceremonial. He died at some unknown date before the end of 1480. Although the plates in this book represent Fouquet only as a painter of panel pictures, it would be inappropriate not to consider his miniatures, for within their few square inches appears all that is most typical of his achievement, and much that is close to the traditions of French art. For here also may be found that realism which attaches the Pietà at Nouans to Courbet's Burial at Ornans. This realism is founded upon a growing belief in the value of man's independent actions, and is a reflection of the individual's more acute sense of himself and his place in the universe. It is an attitude typical of the age, and one which Fouquet shares with his greatest contemporary, the poet François Villon. Fouquet presents the Bible stories in terms of the violent world of his own time, as essentially human conflicts.

Fouquet's miniatures are inhabited by figures and animals which have been most closely observed in their form and movement, and the landscapes bear the mark of local truth. We are immediately convinced by the familiarity of these scenes rather than by their spiritual values. The shepherds by their lonely fire, the carpenters making the cross, the horsemen in St. Martin's train, are the people of his own time and surroundings. This transformation of the ideal and the spiritual into terms of real life is no accident of style, but a deliberate employment of his own experiences and preferences. Fouquet was not a visionary like the Master of Rohan nor a romanticist like the René Master. He was excited by the passing show, by the common habits of humanity, the way they combined into emotional crowds, expressing their passions and their beliefs through a complex pattern of gesture and movement. It is not surprising, therefore, that for Fouquet many of these tiny scenes have been obviously influenced in their presentation by those miracle plays so frequently performed in the open air. One must share Fouquet's interest in human peculiarities, if one is to appreciate to the full the panel paintings reproduced in this book, the two leaves of the Melun Diptych, the Portrait of Charles VII (Plate 14) and the Pietà at Nouans (Plate 18), which has been attributed to the School of Fouquet but is very probably by the master himself. We are accustomed to many interpretations of the Virgin which must disturb our private images, but there is no stranger expression, not only of the Madonna, but of virginity itself, than Fouquet's (Plate 18a). There seems good reason to accept the traditional belief that this woman, with her shaven forehead, her high waist and thin, uncharitable features is indeed Agnes Sorel, the mistress of Charles VII. As in all Fouquet's portraits there is here a curious dichotomy. Not only the figure of the Virgin and the robust Infant Christ, but the red Angels of Day and the blue Angels of Night assert their physical presence with an overpowering plastic realism. They crowd upon the sight within that narrow indefinite space which lies behind the picture surface. And yet the image is remote not only from its devotional theme, but indeed from any immediate contact with our sensuous experience. It has the hieratic aloofness of a Byzantine ikon, but with this is combined the new realism of the fifteenth century.

This same blend of realism and detachment is present in the Portrait of Charles VII, shown, in the whole picture, between the curtains of his box in Church (Plate 14). The figure is forced forward against our sight by the absence of any recession in the background and by the monumental mass of the plum-coloured tunic. The head has been most minutely observed without, it would appear, sympathy or flattery, though the weakness of the features is partly redeemed by the way in which the body seems to be elbowing aside the curtains in a gesture of self-assertion. And yet, like Agnes Sorel, Charles remains inscrutable, the symbol for a man rather than the man himself; a symbol for a man doubtful of his power, his regality and his future.

The pattern of solid forms in space in his *Pietà*, or more obviously within such miniatures as *The Trial at Vendôme*, show that Fouquet was aware of the new spatial resources of the fifteenth century, that the study of perspective had not escaped his notice. In fact, in some of his miniatures it is equally clear that he was informed in the structure of the human anatomy and confident in his power to represent it in any posture or movement. He did not, however, follow the prevailing tendencies in Italy; with him space never became an element to be employed for its own sake, nor were the rules of geometry to be logically pursued. They were always at the service of the story he had to tell, used intuitively to clarify his expression and not to rule it. Again, his knowledge of anatomy and proportion was not influenced by any inclination to idealise the human form. The monumental figures of Masaccio or Piero della Francesca are abstract in comparison with those of Fouquet, which always proclaim their origin and suggest a social environment. Masaccio's Madonna is an idealised figure, but Fouquet's Virgin is clearly a courtesan, whether or not we know that her name is Agnes Sorel. Were it not for his monkish habit and his tonsure, should we realise which of the two figures in the Melun Diptych is St. Stephen and which the painter's patron, Étienne Chevalier? The Saint's features are presented with a more refined realism than the other's, and the face of the unknown sitter has been a more powerful inspiration.

Similarly, the drapery on which the infant Christ and the dead Christ rest is more characteristic, less ideal than the architectural drapery of the Italians. Its thin folds and sharp rhythms are Flemish, and throughout this artist's work there are such hints of his knowledge of Van Eyck and his contemporaries. But if Fouquet is not subject to an Italian idealism he is equally not seduced by fanatical attention to the particularities of nature. He is never pedantic. The accessories in his pictures are warmly and truly observed, but they do not take control. Fouquet adds to this wonderful balance between concepts of the South and percepts of the North, a command of pictorial movement unmatched in the work of any painter of the century. It may be reasonably compared to the human bustle of a Brueghel expressed with some of the refinement of a Watteau. Fouquet is the first clear and defiant personality in the history of French painting. His self-portrait shows a man with the self-assurance of Poussin and the probing vision of Chardin. He became a court painter but in accommodating his style to that patronage, he never lost his fundamental modesty and clear-sightedness. This dispassionate observer of the human scene is also the first of the great French masters.

*

THE OUTSTANDING figure of the fifteenth century after Fouquet was the artist known as the Master of Moulins, the painter of *The Virgin and Child in Glory* in Moulins Cathedral, finished during the last few years of the century (Plate 25). Various other pictures have been attributed to him. Moulins was the ancestral seat of the Bourbons, and this work was commissioned by Pierre II de Beaujeu and by his wife Anne de Beaujeu (Plate 24), the daughter of Louis XI. She is shown with her daughter, Suzanne, and her patroness, St. Anne, while her husband on the opposite leaf is being presented by St. Peter.

There is no more accomplished piece of picture-making in the century. The central panel is a masterpiece of controlled, yet fluent decoration. The pattern of the angels' garments, so tenderly modelled, the unforced variety of their gestures and attitudes, these elements are combined and contrasted with such virtuosity that the picture surface is perpetually alive. As a design it makes Fouquet's *Virgin* from the Melun Diptych seem rough; at the same time it remains a gracious and sophisticated pattern, a trifle sentimental in its details, lacking the bold reality of Fouquet and without the devotional fervour which is expressed in the best work of the School of Avignon. As a sign of the change to this essentially Quattrocento conception, it is interesting to compare the fluent spacious decoration of the Moulins panel with the hieratic order of Enguerrand de Charonton's *Coronation of the Virgin* (Plate 11). The Master of Moulins was also a most sensitive observer of people. He views humanity with that same tenderness which is to be found in the faces and movements of the adoring angels, but his people have not that commanding physical presence which Fouquet gave to his sitters.

Paradoxically, in such portraits as those of *St. Victor and a Donor* (Plate 28) a greater attention to the particularities of the face has led to a much less penetrating observation of character. The two men in this painting are in fact, though different, of the same type, the expression of a courtly gentleness which pervades all the Master's figures. This painter's debt to Flemish art is clearly shown in that early *Nativity* (Plate 26), for the two figures leaning over the stable are taken, with little modification, from a painting by Hugo van der Goes.

\*

THE MOST notable painter of the Northern French School, Simon Marmion, was almost certainly born at Amiens; he worked mainly at Valenciennes where he died in 1489. If Fouquet's illustrations often transcend their tiny scale, Marmion is by nature an illuminator, and his few recognised panel pictures are conceived in terms of a miniature technique—he was called '*le Prince d'Enluminure*'. The scenes from the life of St. Bertin (Plates 33 and 34), his chief panel paintings, have an elegant gaiety and a tender realism which distinguishes even that French art which has been most profoundly influenced by the example of the Low Countries, and they have a clarity and balance which contrasts with those extremes of emotion or realism which so often infect the art of the North.

France had not been able to achieve, in the fifteenth century, that intellectual renaissance which had transformed Italian culture, although individuals like the Duc de Berry and René of Anjou matched their Italian contemporaries in scholarship and a passion for knowledge. There were, however, too few men of commanding intelligence and imagination to drive France forward in such a period of national turbulence.

If one must find an arbitrary date, the French Renaissance may be said to begin in 1494, the year in which Charles VIII marched into Northern Italy. Charles was already devoted to the arts and pursued his tastes with a provincial moderation at his castle at Amboise. The Italian expedition brought him into touch with the most advanced movements in European architecture, sculpture and painting. At the Sforzas' palace at Vizenano he saw work by Bramante, and after his ceremonial entry into Florence, he heard Mass in Brunelleschi's church of San Lorenzo which was decorated with sculptures by Donatello. In fact Charles did not bring back, from what proved to be a disastrous adventure, any painters to serve at his court or any pictures of importance; although some in his train did return not only with a new vision of art but with works by such Italian artists as Perugino, Solario and Fra Bartolommeo.

Charles' successor, Louis XI, was also attracted by the prospect of Italian conquests, and at the time of his brief stay in Milan in 1507 he attempted without success to persuade Leonardo da Vinci to follow him back to France. Louis' chief minister, Cardinal d'Amboise, was even more passionate a connoisseur of the new art. He was for a period in correspondence with Mantegna, whom he called "the greatest painter in the world", while at his castle at Gaillon, which he had transformed into an Italian palace, Solario lived and worked for two years.

But these efforts to Italianise French taste and French art were slight in comparison with the grandiose activities of François I, who came to the throne in 1515 when he was twenty years old. His predecessor had said, "We busy ourselves in vain, that big young fellow will spoil everything"; but at least in the sphere of the arts he succeeded in achieving what they had only aspired to do. In his presence and manner, François was not unlike his English contemporary, Henry VIII; and like him he was a lover of the arts, an amateur humanist with a taste for verse-making and Italian games, a man of ambition and optimism, a patron of painting before all the other arts. Benvenuto Cellini reports him as saying, "I am an amateur and judge of art. I well remember to have inspected all the best works and by the greatest masters of Italy." For, like his two predecessors, he also had great military ambitions and immediately turned his eyes towards Italy. In the first year of his rule he led an army into Lombardy, and after his victory against the Milanese forces at the battle of Marignano, he visited not only Milan, but Bologna and Pavia. According to Vasari he wanted to have Leonardo's *Last Supper* removed from the walls of Santa Maria della Grazie and he certainly at this time invited the painter to France. Leonardo lived at Amboise for the last three years of his life—he died there in 1519—and there is little doubt that the King visited him on several occasions.

Andrea del Sarto was also invited to work in France, and he arrived in the country in 1518. He painted for the King the *Charity* which is now in the Louvre, and the royal collection at Fontainebleau also contained a *Holy Family* by this artist. It is reasonable to believe that the lines which Browning put into del Sarto's mouth are no exaggeration of the welcome which the French court could then give to a Florentine, indeed to any Italian master,

> "I surely then could sometimes leave the ground,
> Put on the glory, Rafael's daily wear,
> In that humane great monarch's golden look."

At the time of his return to Italy in 1519, to that wife with whom he is speaking in the poem, he was commissioned by the King to collect antiquities for him in Rome, but he wasted the money and never came back. François' ambitions went beyond Italian conquests; he coveted the Imperial crown and challenged the power of the Emperor, Charles V. Again, in 1525,

16

he marched into Italy, but with all Europe against him he was defeated at the battle of Pavia and imprisoned for six months in Madrid. Such political failures did not, however, diminish his fervour for the arts. Antique sculpture, bronzes and pictures were continually sent into France from Italy: from Rome, Venice, and Florence—where he employed his own agent, Jean Baptiste de la Palla, who was so zealous on his master's behalf that he incurred the anger of his fellow citizens. François was in touch with Raphael, Michelangelo and Giulio Romano, and he also gave commissions to Sebastiano del Piombo, Pontormo, Bronzino and Salviati, painters of that Mannerist school which was to give its peculiar character to the lavish decorations at Fontainebleau.

The Palace at Fontainebleau was the focus of the King's ambitions; it was to be the Versailles of the sixteenth century. For not only was it the repository of all the treasures which François' taste had attracted into France, not only was it the place where he and his successors exercised their authority as patrons, but it was the centre of the artistic style most typical of the period. The estimates for the rebuilding of this ancient castle were made in 1528 and the building was completed in ten years. In 1531 the first of those Italian artists who were mainly responsible for the decorations in the Palace, Giambattista di Guasparre, named Rosso, arrived from Florence, no doubt through the agency of la Palla, and in the following year he was joined by Francesco Primaticcio, a pupil of Giulio Romano. These artists, with the help of Niccolo dell'Abbate who came from Modena in 1552, and their Italian and French assistants, continued to work at Fontainebleau until the Massacre of St. Bartholomew in 1572 caused a temporary break in the decoration. This work was recommenced under Henry IV, who, now that the chief Italians were dead (Rosso died in 1540 and the other two in 1570), employed French artists such as Toussaint Dubreuil and Ambroise Dubois. Rosso worked in the Galérie de François I, Primaticcio in the Chambre de la Duchesse d'Étampes and the King's Bathing Hall. After the death of François, the latter painted the Ball Room for Henry II with the assistance of dell'Abbate; in the Ulysses Gallery he designed fifty-eight panels devoted to the story of Ulysses, for the walls, and eighteen panels with mythological subjects, for the ceiling.

Rosso and Primaticcio from the beginning conceived an entirely new form of mural decoration, which embodied a mixture of sculptured stucco in high relief with painting set within cartouches, arranged in a rich, overpowering profusion. The motives were those most fashionable in contemporary Italian ornament: antique figures, *putti*, tragic masks, lion's heads, wreaths and swags of leaves, shells and cornucopiæ; the whole, painting and sculpture, moving in harmony with a sinuous rhythm.

In 1540 Primaticcio went back to Rome for a period, returning in 1541 with thirty-three cases of marbles and casts from which bronzes were made. These included the *Laocoön*, and the *Apollo Belvedere*, works which were not only to form the style of such contemporary French sculptors as Jean Goujon, but were to be an inspiration to French artists from then until the time of David. As Rosso had died during his absence, Primaticcio was to become the leader of the Fontainebleau school, and under his influence the style of decoration experienced a considerable change. The massive exuberance of the earlier manner gave way to work of great economy and refinement. Primaticcio decorated the great gallery of Ulysses in the style of Raphael's design at the Vatican, a style which imitated the *grotesques* which had been discovered at the beginning of the century in the ruins of the Baths of Titus. Instead of the deep carvings in the earlier work, the stucco was now applied in low relief and the spaces between the small panels were covered with painted ornament in a lighter and gayer mood.

Among the first works which Rosso had painted for François had been a copy of Michelangelo's *Leda and the Swan*, and his painting was based on that master and upon such painters as Pontormo and Bronzino who followed, and who had transformed Michelangelo's distortions of the human figure and his exaggeration of gesture and expression into something elegant rather than monumental. The work of Rosso, who died by his own hand, was not only exaggerated in its formal mannerisms, but violent and individual in its expression. The excesses of the earlier decorations at Fontainebleau are clearly the work of an unbalanced mind.

It was, in fact, Primaticcio rather than Rosso whose painting formed the Fontainebleau style. Being closer to Parmigiano than to any other artists, he made of Mannerism something elegant rather than emotional, and he established the type of figure which was to people not only the wall painting at Fontainebleau but many of the easel pictures which survive from the period. These figures have small heads. Their features are often strangely hermaphroditic and their expressions have either the blank stare of the marionette or a sinister ambiguity, a certain morbid sweetness. The women have narrow, rounded shoulders, and a sinuous though hardly sensuous rhythm of curves flows from their long waists to their slight, elegant feet. If these Italians brought into French painting a new vocabulary of forms, their paintings at Fontainebleau also introduced into French art a new iconography of classical myth and allegory.

\*

SIDE BY SIDE with this Italianate decorative art, there grew up and flourished a school of portraiture which suddenly burst upon French art in the first years of François' reign and lasted throughout the century; an enormous production from which many paintings and thousands of drawings have survived. Indeed, we can recreate the appearance of French society in the sixteenth century as accurately as we can that of English society in the eighteenth. Portraits of kings and princes, military leaders and great statesmen have proliferated at different times during the past five hundred years—we have only to think of the countless factory-made likenesses of George Washington or Napoleon—but in sixteenth-century France not only were the portraits of royalty and the leaders of the aristocracy duplicated and reduplicated, but it was the fashion to make copies of *all* portraits, as well as to commission drawings of famous men and women of the past—as the Italians had already done. It was also the custom to mount such drawings in albums and to add to them epigrammatic comments. In one such album, which belonged to the wife of one of François I's Grand Masters of France, the aphorisms may have been written by the King himself or at least at his dictation. On one male portrait is inscribed "too small for the cart and too big for the horse", and the drawing of François' mistress, Diane de Poitiers, is labelled with the words "fair to see and virtuous to know".

It is not surprising, given the uniformity and the limitations of such patronage, that the character of portraiture should remain so consistently unvarying throughout the century. Although no pictures can be attributed to him with absolute certainty, Jean Clouet was undoubtedly the founder of this school. His presence at the French court is first recorded in

1516. He was born in the Low Countries and settled first at Tours, where he bore the title of *Valet de Chambre* and where he married a jeweller's daughter. He then worked in Paris, where he died some time during the first six months of 1541. It is not known when his more famous son, François, was born; the first evidence of his existence appears in a document dated 1541 when, like his father, he was holding the office of royal *Valet de Chambre* and *Brevetaire*.

By the reign of Henry II a definite school of French portraiture had arisen, with such names as Germain Lemannier, Nicolas Denisot, Jean Serpin and Étienne Dumoutier. François Clouet died in 1572, not long after the Massacre of St. Bartholomew. The limitations of the Clouets' portraiture, and indeed of all the portrait paintings and drawings of the period, are precisely those imposed by the aristocratic patronage which they so faithfully and so modestly served. Like the portraits of Fouquet, they are pictures of types, not studies of individual psychology but at the same time they never make such a penetrating analysis of the sitter's features as can be found in the portraits of that master. Nor have the figures that strong physical presence which Fouquet projected on to his panels. These sixteenth-century portraits display a great refinement of drawing and craftsmanship. However flattering they may have been, at least they do not excite admiration or awe for their subjects by any of the grosser conceits of fashionable portraiture. Even the picturesque magnificence of the *Equestrian Portrait of François I* (Plate 37), in which the head is the least important and least expressive feature, is quite acceptable, for the painting of the armour and the harness is achieved without any vulgar virtuosity. These paintings have a reserve not altogether appropriate to a society which displayed very little.

It is when one sets the work of the Clouets beside the comparable portraits of Holbein that their limitations become apparent. The Clouets' power to express the structure of the human head is elementary by comparison, for Holbein's heads, even when they belong to people of an undistinguished intelligence or temperament, hold us by their individual presence. Holbein extracted the most from the restrictions of the bust portrait, contriving such a subtle pattern of shapes and intervals, that the architecture of each of his pictures may be submitted to the closest individual study. The Clouets could seldom animate the rectangles within which their figures were set. The fine *Portrait of Pierre Quthe* (Plate 36), which represents the refinement of Clouet's observation at its best, still betrays a putting together of objects. All such pictures were made not direct from the sitter, but from preliminary drawings in black or red chalk or in a mixture of the two, and here the book and the curtain obtrude as objects added to fill spaces.

The other portrait painter of the period was Corneille de Lyon, a native of the Hague who settled at Lyons in about 1536. On the occasion of the accession of Henry II he became one of his court painters. Corneille's portraits, like that of the boy in Plate 39, are all of them small panels, where the head and shoulders are painted with a nervous delicacy against flat blue or green backgrounds. His touch was more broken than the consistent enamel of the Clouets, and his contours less severe. At first it may appear as if these little paintings show more insight than those of the Clouets, as if they are, in fact, closer to the vital temperament of the sitters, but that is to be deceived by their slight technical mannerisms. To think that their more agitated touch contains a deeper inquiry into the human personality is akin to believing that Hals is a more profound observer than Velasquez.

We must add to the Italianate decorations of Rosso, Primaticcio and their French followers, and to the countless portraits and portrait albums, a group of paintings which, even more

19

intimately than these, reflect the tastes and indulgences of the time—the taste for classical literature and history, the luxury and licentiousness of the court and the aristocracy, and those sinister intrigues which came into French politics with the marriage of Henry II to Catherine de Medici. Prior to the arrival of the visiting Italian painters at Fontainebleau, and before their art obtained a predominant influence, François had collected Flemish paintings by or in the manner of Hieronymus Bosch. Some of these pictures represented scenes from Italian and French comedies, others were based upon fashionable contemporary jokes against aged lovers. After 1560 another series of paintings begins to emerge in which the stylistic influence is Venetian rather than Flemish. They are mainly devoted to a glorification of feminine beauty—their subjects include *The Bath of Diana, The Bath of the Nymphs, Venus, Diana and Actæon*—and one has been ascribed to François Clouet. There are also portraits of Roman ladies and courtesans (Plates 40–43).

All these pictures have a strange and somewhat sinister ambiguity. They are full of unusual encounters and allusions, no doubt as transparent in their own time as the gauze draperies which so temptingly reveal the figure of *Sabina* (Plate 41). Some of this ambiguity is due to the fact that many of the nymphs and goddesses were aristocratic ladies and royal mistresses in thin disguise. The long-limbed *Diana* (Plate 40) is Diane de Poitiers—mistress of François I, and the ladies in the bath (Plate 43) are Gabrielle d'Estrées, mistress of Henry IV, and her sister. The conception of these figures is both sensuous and detached, for although the painters were expected to celebrate the sexual attraction of their sitters (a contemporary poet wrote "Comme elle est, tire la, s'il le plait, Lui découvrant ses montagnes de lait") there is in the pictures none of that frank, warm eroticism which Boucher was to provide a hundred and fifty years later for a similarly licentious society. The allusiveness of these pictures has even invaded the landscapes of Niccolo dell'Abbate, who probably introduced this kind of painting into French art. What is this strange encounter of a lady and her lover in the hayfield, an encounter which seems so inappropriate and is indeed so detached from the peasants at their daily work (Plate 44)? And how oddly the mannerist distortions of all the figures and the horses combine to give a sense of foreboding and unreality to this gentle pastoral. In the same way the people in the shadowy room (Plate 45), so commonly employed, seem to be conspirators in some tragedy of blood.

Considering the energy and ambition of François I and his successors, the achievement of French sixteenth-century painting is slight, and the most enduring works of the time are those which are the least pretentious, the portraits of the Clouets and their school. The intro-duction of foreign art and foreign artists did not strengthen or create a national school, and the twenty years before the death of Henry IV in 1610 are amongst the most unproductive in the history of French art. The finest poets of the century were able to achieve a fruitful synthesis of the forms and themes of Greek and Latin literature, and the tradition of native poetry. None of the painters and only few of the sculptors and architects could claim a like success; they were equally far from approaching the inventive genius of Rabelais or the urbane irony of Montaigne. It was in the following century that the synthesis which the sixteenth century had so passionately sought was achieved.

The Edict of Nantes of 1598, giving freedom of worship to French Protestants, was not only to end a struggle which had threatened, more seriously than the disasters of the Italian campaign, the unity gained by France in the fifteenth century; it was also to announce the most brilliant period in French history. This brilliance was founded upon order, discipline, efficiency and the application of reason to practical affairs. In public life its representatives are Richelieu, Colbert and Louis XIV himself; in philosophy, Descartes and Pascal; in literature, Racine and Corneille before any others. In painting it found its finest expression in the rational and profoundly philosophical genius of Poussin and the classical lyricism of Claude. Its most typical monuments were the *Académie Royale de Peinture et Sculpture* and the Palace of Versailles.

*

FIRST we must consider a group of painters—the brothers Le Nain, Dumesnil de la Tour and Baugin—who stand outside the main currents of the period, who were to have no influence upon the achievements of the next two centuries, and whose work was formed not by the ideal and epic art of Italy, but by the popular, descriptive pictures of the Low Countries.

We have already seen that there had been a spasmodic taste in the previous century, among royal or aristocratic patrons, for pictures of low life or the strange inventions of such artists as Hieronymus Bosch, and there had certainly been a continuous popular demand for drawings and prints devoted to such themes, French as well as Flemish. In Holland the new bourgeois patronage had helped to create the characteristic art of a Teniers or a Paul Potter, and this demand had its slighter counterpart in France. Except in special circumstances, foreign artists were prevented from exhibiting or selling their work in Paris by the rules of the Maîtrise or the Guild of St. Luke, a body of artists whose royal charter had been granted in 1391 by Charles VI.

In the region of Saint Germain des Prés, then outside the city boundaries, there existed, however, a colony of Dutch and Flemish painters—some of whom had been assistants to Rubens when he was working for Marie de Medici—which had its own independent guild of artists and a place of annual exhibition in the Saint Germain Fair. It seems likely that it was at this fair that the three brothers Le Nain first made their reputation, for the eldest of them, Antoine, was Master of the Guild of Saint Germain. It was for long believed that the three brothers worked together on all their paintings—where these are signed no christian names are indicated—but during the last forty years the surviving works have been divided among them and their individual characteristics determined. All three were born at Laon, Antoine in 1588, Louis about 1593 and Mathieu in 1607, the last two being made founder members of the Academy in 1648, the year in which the two elder brothers died; Mathieu was to survive until 1677.

What are the characteristics common to these three artists apart from the bourgeois plainness of their themes? Most obvious is the recurrent and almost monotonous simplicity of their designs. The figures are disposed with an equal emphasis across the surface of the canvas, generally within a very narrow and roughly defined space. Where the subject does carry with it some suggestion of a deeper space, as in Plate 49, there is no attempt to draw the eye into any complex spatial pattern, and the figures at a distance are displayed with as much clarity and accent as those in the foreground, often, indeed, with such a distortion of their scale, that the customary sense of a hieratic composition is preserved. The figures are always still; their occasional gestures are restrained, almost hesitant. It is as if they had been surprised at their daily pursuits by some strangers of high degree who had reduced them to a state of modest, but friendly embarrassment. The expressions in these people's faces are invariably unassuming and sympathetic; the prevailing mood is one of stoic contentment and reserve. The figures seem to be detached from one another by their own calm introspection and at the same time profoundly linked by the ties of family or friendship. The paint is appropriate to this sober vision of life. It is solid and firm like the matière of Géricault's paintings of mad people or of Courbet's pictures—and, incidentally, it was Courbet's friend, Champfleury, who rediscovered these artists after a lapse of two centuries. Their colour has a similar restraint, with a preponderance of stony or metallic greys, sober browns and chalky whites.

But if the three brothers were much alike in their attitude to society, their individual gifts and to some extent their temperaments were very different. Antoine was the least skilful of the three. As Plate 47 shows, he never managed to acquire a knowledge of human proportions, nor the ability to dispose his figures coherently even within the restricted space he made behind the canvas. In fact, he resorted to the archaic device of placing the background figures higher up the canvas than their true position demanded, and the head is often upon a nearer plane than the rest of the figure. His portraits have a gentle and sympathetic liveliness, but the faces are only slightly differentiated, the same features occurring again and again. The folds in the drapery are not only tentatively constructed, but have no architectural order.

Mathieu was more fluent, more refined and came closer than either of his brothers to those Dutch artists who had so strongly influenced all three. Louis is, by far, the finest artist. He could make a monumental grandeur out of the simple Le Nain vocabulary of picture making. The figures in the *Peasant Family* (Plate 48) have an over-powering presence, that kind of super-real presence which Chardin could give to a marmite or Cézanne to the Mont Ste Victoire; he possessed that power, given only to great artists, to animate the material of their art and to transcend those critical categories of which lesser artists always remind us. We remember that Antoine and Mathieu are painters of genre, as we remember, in the face of his work, that Charles le Brun was a history painter and forget that Poussin is. Louis had, first of all, a superb intuitive command of interval. In this picture, which is one of his finest achievements, there is not only the subtle disposition of the four main figures with the counter-balance of the minor ones, but there are the spaces which lie between these figures with their own commanding tension. Unlike his two brothers, Louis used chiaroscuro with absolute confidence, not only to unify his designs but also to endow the scene with a positive mood and atmosphere.

If the identity of the brothers Le Nain is shadowy and their biographies poorly documented, the life of Georges Dumesnil de la Tour is even more difficult to track. He was born at Lunéville, where he died in 1652. Among those we know to have commissioned work from him were Louis XIII, the Governor of Nancy and Duke Charles IV of Lorraine. It is obvious that his paintings, all of which represent scenes illuminated by candle or torchlight, were influenced by that Neapolitan school of painters known as the 'Tenebrosi' and by the work of the Dutchman, Gerard Honthorst, who introduced this kind of picture into Northern Europe. This concentration upon a particular form of lighting had been derived from similar effects in the art of Caravaggio and from Raphael's painting, *The Liberation of St. Peter*. Such an interest may easily lead to empty mannerism, seeing that it is essentially a problem of technique, or at least an incidental aspect of appearances.

The history of European art is full of equally fruitless experiments with ideas detached from the whole world of knowledge and visual experience; from the breadth and richness of the great artists. The trivialities which Seurat's followers so often made of pointillism is an obvious case in the history of French painting, and de la Tour's successful conquest of the slight device of artificial lighting is in many ways comparable with Seurat's control of his own technical devices, for both artists were armed with similar resources. Both possessed an acute sense of pattern. Both shared a tendency to exaggerate the geometry of the human body by a simplification of its contours and its modelling. Both reduced the complexity of planes in the figure to a comparatively few flat shapes by using a strict pattern of lights and darks with which to carve out the forms. In the case of de la Tour, the sharp light of the candle or the torch makes this simplification appear more natural than it is, less arbitrary indeed than the distortion in Seurat's pictures where the light is generally even and undramatic. The peculiar force of the St. Sebastian picture (Plate 54) is due to these characteristics, and above all to the defiant severity with which the arrow sprouts from the flattened surface of the diaphragm. This is as powerful an image of destruction and finality as can be found anywhere in art. In isolation the profile of the woman with the torch, the tense convexity of the forehead flowing into the equally severe concavity of the breast and waist might have come from the *Dimanche sur la Grande Jatte*. Like Seurat, de la Tour was extremely sensitive to the significant gesture, though with him the gesture not only gives a greater reality to the physical presence of his figures—as in the characteristic actions of reading in Plate 53, and of the shielding of the candlelight or the hesitant hand raised to the shepherd's cap, both in the *Adoration of the Shepherds* (Plate 52)—but is often a most restrained indication of mood, nowhere more finely revealed than in Plate 54.

De la Tour's command of significant pattern has, in the past twenty-five years, revived our interest and raised our estimation of his painting. But there is another characteristic of his art which must appeal to contemporary taste: that clarity of vision which gives an almost human presence to the incidental objects in his pictures—the book, for example, the skull and the scissors in Plate 53. The same synthesis of realism and abstraction is found in the *Still Life* of Baugin (Plate 46), a picture painted in about 1630.

While the years after Louis XIV's assumption of power were to see the building and decoration of his palace at Versailles, the first half of the century was no less a time of considerable activity, particularly in Paris, which was transformed during these years from a mediæval town to a modern city—a city fit to be the capital of the new nation state which was arising to the order of France's kings and cardinals. Marie de Medici built the Luxembourg Palace, Richelieu the Palais Royal, and Louis XIII made great additions to the Louvre. The nobility and rich bourgeois built their splendid hotels near the Luxembourg and in the quarters of St. Antoine, the Marais and the Île St. Louis. The religious revival which took place as a result of Richelieu's tolerant and enlightened ecclesiastical policy led to the building of a host of new churches in the city.

Such developments created a demand, not only for the employment of native artists, but for a particular kind of painting, an art which could be decorative and at the same time didactic, monumental and yet gracious. Such works were to be supplied most competently by Simon Vouet, his pupil Eustache le Sueur and others such as François Perrier and Laurent de la Hyre. The taste for an Italian style so firmly established in the previous century by François I and his successors was to be sustained. French painters were expected at least to have completed their education in Italy, and to be able in consequence to reproduce the themes, the style and the mannerisms of Raphael, of Italian Baroque or of the Neapolitan naturalists. Vouet's father had been decorative painter working under the patronage of Henry IV. He visited Constantinople, Venice and Rome, and was in Italy for thirteen years altogether, working in the Vatican and the Doria Palace at Genoa; he was elected a Prince of the Roman Academy of St. Luke. In 1627 he returned to France by royal command and was appointed 'Premier Peintre du Roi', by Louis XIII. He made decorations for the Louvre and the Luxembourg Palace and for many of the new hotels and churches, and was commissioned by Richelieu. He was indeed to occupy as dominant a position during the '30's and '40's as his pupil, Le Brun, was to do in the '60's and '70's (he was continuously employed and was surrounded by a great number of assistants and apprentices). His art is an anthology of Italian devices. He tried to combine the monumentality of Raphael and his followers with the richness and grace of the Venetians. *Wealth* (Plate 56), one of a series of four allegorical figures in the Louvre, is a proof of his ability to make a bold decorative gesture and to order his grandiose designs with some sense of rhythm and some tenderness of observation.

Vouet's pupil, Eustache le Sueur, born in Paris in 1616, was an artist of much smaller pretensions and less influence. Unlike his master, he never visited Italy, but his nickname, 'The French Raphael', as well as the evidence of his painting suggest the first source of his inspiration. He also worked consistently though with less material success, for churches, monasteries and hotels, including the Carthusian monastery in Paris, for which he painted twenty-two pictures of the life of St. Bruno. Vouet had striven after the grand idealism of sixteenth-century Italian art; but Le Sueur, perhaps because he had remained at home, presented his themes, on whatever scale they were, in more human terms. However artificial or derivative may be the total design, its parts are presented with an almost tentative restraint. Indeed his best picture, *The Mass of St. Martin of Tours*, painted for the Abbaye of Marmoutier, is among the most moving and least affected religious pictures of the period. It is typical that the three Muses in Plate 55, *Melpomene, Erato and Polyhymnia*, should be conceived with Raphael in the artist's mind and yet with all that master's pagan idealism reduced to a French intimacy.

Neither Vouet nor Le Sueur are among France's greatest painters but their work shows, at least, some progress in the French assimilation of the Italian High Renaissance. These painters and others of the first half of the seventeenth century could employ Italian methods with great competence and with some national individuality, even if they could not transcend the necessary limitations of eclecticism. They served their time admirably and established some valuable examples for the future. That Italian and Classical influences could be transformed into a new, a unique and above all, a French synthesis, was left to the greatest painter of the century, Nicolas Poussin.

*

POUSSIN is the greatest representative of the finest virtues of French painting, of that French gift for assimilating creatively the influences of other artists and other schools, the power to exercise reason with passion. Poussin was born in Normandy in 1594, his father having served as a soldier in the armies of Henry IV and Charles IX. Before going to Paris in 1612 he had worked in the studio of a provincial painter at Rouen. Having encountered in the capital the Italian drawings and engravings after such masters as Raphael, Poussin was encouraged to journey to Rome; but twice through lack of money he was forced to return, though on the first occasion he did make his way as far as Florence.

When, in 1624, he finally did arrive in Rome, he studied antique reliefs and sculpture and worked in the studio of Domenichino. It was through Cardinal Barberini that he met one of the city's leading antiquaries, Cassiano del Pozzo, who almost certainly employed Poussin to make drawings from ancient relics. In 1640 he was commanded to return to Paris, where he worked for Louis XIII and Richelieu, one of his commissions being to make decorations for the Long Gallery of the Louvre. After two years, however, finding the life at court most uncongenial he returned to Rome where he remained until his death in 1665.

There is no better estimate of Poussin's genius than the essay 'On a Landscape of Nicholas Poussin' by William Hazlitt, from which the following lines are taken:

". . . he could give to the scenery of his historic fables that unimpaired look of original nature, full, solid, large, luxuriant, teeming with life and power; or deck it with all the pomp of art, with temples and towers and mythologic groves. His pictures denote a foregone conclusion. He applies nature to his purposes, works out her images according to the standard of his thoughts, embodies high fictions . . . With a laborious and a mighty grasp, he put nature into the mould of the ideal and the antique; and was among painters what Milton was among poets. There is in both something of the same stiffness, the same pedantry, the same elevation, the same grandeur, the same mixture of art and nature, the same richness of borrowed materials, the same unity of character. He was a painter of ideas . . . There is a significance, a consciousness of what he does beyond any other painter . . ."

"He was a painter of ideas." Poussin was in no sense merely an illustrator of historical, mythological or religious themes; he was an artist who found not only a pictorial symbol for the episodes he chose, but developed through such episodes a clear philosophy. Even his landscapes, either the earlier monumental compositions such as the *Orion*, to which Hazlitt refers, the two pictures which represent the death and burial of Phocion, or the later ones such as those reproduced in Plates 57 and 58, profoundly augment the expression of the incidents they contain. Like his great contemporary, the dramatist Racine, Poussin used his pictures to present in microcosm the fundamental passions and ideals of mankind. As Milton extended the few verses of Genesis into his monumental religious epic, Poussin gave to the story of the *Golden Calf*, the *Finding of Moses* or even one of his early *Bacchanals* (Plate 59), a significance which went far beyond the limits of these stories.

A "richness of borrowed materials". Poussin did not hesitate to employ all that he found to his liking in the past and present art of Italy, the example of his master Domenichino, of his great predecessors Titian and Raphael, or those relics of antiquity of which he had such a deep and scholarly appreciation. Indeed he was capable, as few other artists have been, of making a vital re-creation of the classical forms which he adopted. The *Bacchanals*, all but one of which were painted before his interlude in Paris, are compounded of forms and motives from Titian's *Bacchanals* and spatial organisation and rhythms which he found in classical reliefs.

The seventeenth-century tragedies of Racine and Corneille were not invariably based upon classical themes, but were strictly bound by the unities of time, place and action laid down by Aristotle in his 'Poetics'. Such restrictions and the dignified alexandrines in which the verse was cast give a wonderful clarity and grandeur to the actions and passions of these plays. There is in the legalistic arguments in which Corneille's characters discuss their most intimate relationships, or in the elevated and formal speeches of Racine's lovers, something of that stiffness and pedantry which Hazlitt found so moving in the gestures and movements of Poussin's figures, that same passionate restraint which intensifies the clash of characters. Poussin expressed this principle in a letter to his friend and patron, Paul de Fréart. "Our wise ancient Greeks," he wrote, "inventors of all beautiful things, found several modes by means of which they produced marvellous effects. This word mode means actually the rule or the measure and forms which serve us in our production. This rule constrains us not to exaggerate by making us act in all things with a certain restraint and moderation; and, consequently, this restraint and moderation is nothing more than a certain determined manner or order and includes the procedure by which the object is preserved in its essence." This belief in the efficacy of order and of reason led him indeed to postulate in his pictures those rules of composition and expression which were to be the basis of French Academic teaching.

André Gide once wrote that a classical work is beautiful by virtue of its subjugated romanticism. The many passages of tender insight and vision which occur so frequently in Poussin's works (for example the flowered trellis against the sky in Plate 59a), are all the more powerful for being set within so austere a framework. Poussin was the greatest of French classical painters. He exercised those principles of pictorial composition to which any of his contemporaries had access with a passion and an integrity which none of them could rival. Those who see in his art only the highest expression of the academic, neglect to observe that for him formal order, even indeed some pedantry of design, is almost invariably a way of expressing with absolute clarity and economy experiences of the profoundest intellectual, imaginative and visual reality. His paintings find perhaps their closest counterpart in the music of Johann Sebastian Bach, and the more explicit romanticism of a Beethoven or a Delacroix should not be brought to their judgment.

To turn from Poussin to Claude is to move from an art of pure reason to one in which sensation and intuition have also been allowed to interfere. Claude was, officially, a German, for at the time of his birth in 1600 Lorraine was a part of the empire, and when twelve he was living at Breisgau, with an elder brother who gave him his first instruction in painting. When he went to Italy at the age of fifteen, he worked first in the Naples studio of the Cologne painter, Gottfried Wols, and then in Rome with Agostino Tassi. After twelve years of somewhat aimless and unsuccessful travelling in North Italy, Austria and France, he finally settled in Rome in 1627 where he remained until his death in 1682. For the next ten years his work attracted little notice, but from the 1640's he was never without employment and his paintings were eagerly acquired by collectors all over Europe, but particularly in England.

Agostino Tassi, with whom Claude worked for nine years and who instructed him in perspective, painted, among other things, harbour scenes and pictures of shipping; and Claude, too, was mainly engaged on subjects of this nature and with Roman landscapes until he reached the age of fifty. Thereafter his energies were devoted to landscapes animated by biblical or mythological incidents. Claude had none of Poussin's profound intelligence, nor his intellectual seriousness. And if, in comparison with a Constable or a Monet, his landscapes seem artificial and ideal, he was like them dependent, as Poussin never allowed himself to be, upon his sensations and above all upon his sensation of light.

Light is, perhaps, the least expressive of all the elements in painting, but none is more powerful in its operation, for it can destroy the power of local colour and threaten the illusion of space and volume. Claude was the most ardent student of light in the history of European art before the nineteenth century. Like Constable and the Impressionists, he gave his attention to the changing effects which appear at different times of the day. Any concentration upon the properties of light must involve the painter in compromises and rejections. Monet was to make his compromise between light and local colour, and largely to reject the expression of solid form and of space. Claude made no such compromise between light and space, but modified, as did all landscape painters before Constable, the natural colour within a landscape. In his paintings, even when they are clean, the bright greens of spring and summer are diffused. The exquisite harmonies of a Claudian landscape are achieved within a very narrow range of colour.

In an impressionist painting light does not lie upon the surface of objects, but seems rather to have been absorbed into them and then thrown back into our eyes. In a Claude, however, the light lies like a veil over the surface of things and we are aware of their permanent identity beneath this temporary clothing of luminosity. In an impressionist picture—compare the Claudes (Plates 66–68) here with the Monets (Plates 128 and 129) or the Sisley (Plate 130) —there is always the element of change, of movement; indeed, by suggestion, of time itself. The cloud is about to shift and the shadows to alter their pattern. But Claude, like Poussin, presents us with a world fixed eternally in the present, bound by the classical unities with no hint of a past or a future to disturb the ideal balance of elements within the picture frame. Claude was not, like Poussin, a student of classical antiquity, and his works have none of the latter's historical truth; but in their own more intuitive way they offer a meditation upon classical themes which is equally compelling and suggestive. Most of his landscapes are animated by incidents chosen from the Bible, mythology or history, but these are only secondary; all the more so because Claude never commanded the structure of the human figure, and often, indeed, the figures were painted in by other artists.

As Claude's work matured, not only did he come, within the terms of his conventions, closer to the reality of nature, but the construction of his pictures became increasingly coherent. In his earlier pictures and, particularly in such harbour scenes as Plate 68, with their architectural foreground directing the eye so positively into the distance, the scene is regularly disposed as if within a box, the horizon marking its farthest limits quite abruptly, and the sky itself being an impenetrable but refulgent plane. One's eye makes its gradual advance through the picture, not so much by means of a slow transition from accent to accent and plane to plane, but because the light shines so powerfully from the backcloth of the sky that it hinders the eye's advance from foreground to background. In his mature paintings (Plate 67 is a superb example) a different entry may be made into the spaces behind the picture frame. Claude's skies have ceased to be impenetrable. The eye still does not pass beyond the horizon into infinity as it may in a Turner, but it does sink into a sky which does not repel the sight. The transition from plane to plane becomes more subtle so that the eye slides over the surface of rocks, water and foliage without any lack of continuity. Even the buildings and stones have no rough edges, so subtly are they enveloped in light. To pass through one of Poussin's heroic landscapes is to scramble over the ruins of some splendidly carved temple. Our passage through a Claude is like gliding through the calmest of water. As he grew older Claude's landscapes also seemed to be more and more influenced by that tender perception of nature which is the glory of his landscape drawings.

\* 

THE GREATEST portraitist of the period was Philippe de Champaigne, a Fleming born in Brussels in 1602, but trained in France and a resident there for most of his life. He was a life-long friend of Poussin who, during his short stay in France, found him work in the Luxembourg Palace under the Court painter, Duchesne. But although he received many commissions for religious and decorative compositions, working in St. Germain d'Auxerrois, in Rouen Cathedral and for Richelieu at the Palais Royal and the Sorbonne, it is his portraits which have secured de Champaigne his reputation. He was a friend of Richelieu, and the severity of his uncompromising realism was a most appropriate instrument for recording his Cardinal friend's austere appearance and the rational strength of his intellect. Indeed, one can be sure that the traditional image of Richelieu which subsequent generations have derived from de Champaigne's portraits is close to the truth. In later life domestic troubles caused the painter to withdraw from the official world, and he became closely associated with the Jansenists, whose near-Calvinist doctrine of predestination and salvation by grace made a profound appeal to his mystical temperament. His daughter became a nun at the Jansenist headquarters of Port-Royal, and it is from this last period of his life that the portrait here reproduced (Plate 64) derives. This almost certainly represents Madame Le Maître who became Mère Catherine de Saint-Jean in Port-Royal, and here again de Champaigne's noble seriousness has found an ideal subject.

As the seventeenth century saw the transformation of Paris into a modern city, so also it saw the emergence of France as a great nation state. That same policy of centralisation which Richelieu practised in the field of government was applied to the arts. In 1635 Richelieu founded the Académie Française. Cardinal Mazarin who continued Richelieu's policy after the latter's death and during the youth of Louis XIV, himself died in 1661, the first year of Louis' personal rule; and, like his great predecessor, he handed on his responsibilities and his ideals to one of his closest followers, Colbert. It was Colbert who consummated that academic system which had been inaugurated twelve years before in 1648, when the *Académie de Peinture et Sculpture* had been founded. During the previous century, when so many foreign artists were employed in court, and there enjoyed the privileges which the King could grant to his *Valet de Chambre* and *Brevetaires*, the Guild of St. Luke had several times obtained the confirmation of their rights. But in 1646, the Guild not only asked for a further guarantee of their own position, but requested Parliament in their interest to limit the number of court painters. This action raised the opposition of the *Brevetaires* and in two groups, one of which included the young Charles le Brun who had just returned from Italy, they made a formal request to the King for the establishment of an Academy.

They argued as other artists in Italy had argued in the sixteenth century when, in Florence and Rome, a similar conflict of interests had arisen, that it was essential to the future dignity of their profession, for *les arts nobles* to be separated from *les arts méchaniques*. They maintained that the status of the arts in France would suffer if the entry of foreign artists and foreign works of art were forbidden. Their petition also presented a scheme of art education which would offer a thorough training in architecture, geometry, perspective, arithmetic, anatomy, astronomy and history.

These proposals were in the main accepted; the foundation meeting of the new academy was held in February 1648 and, in spite of the determined counter-attacks of the guilds, it secured Parliament's confirmation of its privileges later in the same year. Within a few months the King not only promised an annual grant of £1,000, but also offered rooms at the *Collège Royale de l'Université*.

In 1656, the Academy moved into a suite of rooms in the Louvre. Five years later, when Colbert came into power he immediately devoted his energies to strengthening the Academy's position, to giving it an absolute authority; to this end, in 1663, he made it obligatory for all court painters to join. The arts in fact were not to be excluded from that vast scheme of political, social and economic centralisation which was destroying the last traces of provincial and local autonomy brought about by the similar policies of Richelieu and Mazarin.

Just as it was easier to govern a country's political destinies when her local laws, customs and loyalties had been abolished, so it was easier for art to serve the royal will, as it soon would be called upon to do, when all artists of merit were under one surveillance. The artist was offered an unprecedented social position and prestige on the one hand and on the other was bound to sacrifice a great deal of his independence. With the same end in view Colbert founded during the following ten years Academies of the Dance, of Science, of Music, of Architecture and of '*Inscriptions et Belles-Lettres*'.

Colbert, then, gave the Academy its power, its place in society and its mission; but it was the painter Charles Le Brun who gave it its æsthetic, for he had that zeal which lies at the heart of an ambitious man. Le Brun, who was born in Paris in 1619, was the son of a sculptor and worked first in the studio of François Perrier and then with Simon Vouet. With an opportunism which was to characterise his whole career, he presented to Richelieu a painting representing the glory of the Cardinal in allegorical form. Not only commissions but an introduction to the King followed, and by the age of nineteen Le Brun was a '*Peintre du Roi*'.

In 1642 he accompanied Poussin on his return to Rome, where in 1645 he gained fame and success with his *Horatius Cocles Defending Rome* which he exhibited there anonymously. On his return to Paris in 1646 he was able to secure an appointment as one of Louis XIV's court painters, and soon obtained commissions for churches and convents, which included a picture for Notre Dame. He also gained the friendship of the most famous collectors and connoisseurs of the time, including the German banker Jabach, whose portrait he painted and whose Paris hotel contained the splendid collection of paintings acquired so cheaply by Colbert for the King. The portrait of his patron Chancellor Séguier (Plate 69) is one of the most satisfactory examples of his rhetoric.

The first evidence of Le Brun's striking energy and virtuosity as a designer of decorations is shown in his connection with Nicolas Fouquet, *Surintendent des Finances*. At Fouquet's Château de Vaux he painted a series of allegorical compositions, designed fêtes and firework displays, and founded a tapestry factory. It was here that he became acquainted with Cardinal

29

Mazarin who introduced him to Louis XIV, and for this king he painted a picture, *Alexander and the Family of Darius,* which is now in the Louvre. When in 1661 Mazarin died and Fouquet fell from favour, Le Brun was quick to transfer his allegiance once again—this time to Colbert —with the result that in 1662 he was made '*Premier Peintre du Roi*'.

From then until Colbert's death in 1683 he served him and the King as the designer-in-chief of those vast schemes which were to be the lasting memorial of Louis' power and ambition; though, unlike François I, *le roi soleil* was no lover of the arts, but only devoted to his own glorification. Le Brun decorated Colbert's Château de Sceaux and designed its fountains and gardens which were to have their own influence upon the work of Le Nôtre at Versailles. But the centre of his activities was the King's new palace which was in the most exact sense Louis' court, for here lived five thousand of the French nobility, with five thousand others lodging in the neighbourhood, in a style which was to match the magnificence of the Palace decorations and ceremonies.

At Versailles, Le Brun designed the *Grand Escalier,* the *Salons de la Guerre et de la Paix* and the *Grands Galéries des Glaces.* There he painted thirty allegorical compositions each of which celebrated some glorious occasion in the King's life—paintings in which all the apparatus of classical mythology and all that pictorial machinery which his receptive intellect had learnt in Italy were put logically at the service of his master. These paintings are both grand and absurd, grand because they are the work on a large scale of an artist who was fully educated in the grand manner; absurd because their conventions and the æsthetic upon which these were based had only a temporary significance, depending entirely upon a now impossible acceptance of their standards. But besides being the creator of these paintings and the overseer of a host of assistants, Le Brun was also in charge of other masters and of quite different undertakings. The sculptor Coysevox and the great garden designer Le Nôtre were among those who worked at his bidding.

Le Brun's works are in the strictest sense academic. They are serviceable, and although they are on a grand scale, entirely unadventurous. Their inadequacies derive exactly from those academic doctrines they embody. The Italian Academies of the sixteenth century and the French Academy made the important distinction between the artist as craftsmen and the artist as follower of an intellectual profession. The painter or the sculptor was to become the equal of the man of intellect because to a command of manual skills he had to bring the attainments of the savant. Behind the organisation and the curriculum lay the belief that art is the expression of principles which may be analysed and communicated. Art depends upon knowledge—mainly a knowledge of the masters of the past—and not so much upon individual inspiration. The creative process is much the same thing as the rational process. As Fréart de Chambray wrote in his *Idées de la Perfection de la Peinture,* a real knowledge of art can only be had by those "*qui examinent et jugent les choses à les manières des Géomètres*". There are, consequently, laws of pictorial composition and expression which have only to be discovered to be acted upon. Indeed, one might transfer from the second book of Descartes' famous *Discours de la Méthode,* that gospel of seventeenth-century rationalism, those passages in which he displays such principles of his philosophy as, ". . . Never to accept anything for true which I did not clearly know to be such . . . to comprise nothing more in my judgment than what was presented to my mind so clearly and distinctly as to exclude all grounds of doubt . . . to divide each of the difficulties under its own examination into as many parts as possible . . . to conduct my thoughts in such order that by beginning with objects the simplest and easiest to know I might ascend little by little, and, as it were, step by step, to the knowledge of the more complex . . ."

The students of the new Academy, who still had to learn in their masters' studios how to paint, carve or model, moved progressively from copying the drawings of the professors, to drawing from plaster casts and originals of classical sculpture, and thence to a study of the living model, a study which could by law be gained only within the Academy. Lectures were also given on perspective, geometry and anatomy. More important even than these aspects of the curriculum, however, were the discourses and conferences founded upon the lectures given at the Roman Academy by Zuccari; but unlike those, they were intended for students as well as for trained artists. By means of these lectures the student might hear, and later perhaps read, those 'préceptes positifs' which Colbert valued so highly. It was the custom in these lectures to analyse a picture—often a work by Poussin—according to such categories as invention, proportion, colour and expression. Out of these analyses and discussions certain ruling principles of art were to grow.

Works of art were divided into a hierarchy of value, with still life as the least important, then, in ascending order, landscape, animal pictures, portraits and—of predominant value— histories. It was the essence of these history pictures, the typical academic productions for the next two centuries, that they should be noble in their conception and didactic in their purpose. Le Brun's allegories might be considered to serve the academic ideal. Within such paintings the proportions of the figures were to be regulated by those found in classical sculpture, and by following the classical examples the irregularities of nature were to be corrected. At one conference Le Brun laid down rules and methods for the proper portrayal of human feelings and passions, a system closely related to the ideas in Descartes' *Traité des Passions de l'Âme.* Drawing was more important than colour, and, ideally, the conception of the figure should be sculptural: paint was to be handled with a reasonable moderation. Such was the body of artistic theory which dominated the first years of the Academy's existence and which was the source of Le Brun's own painting. But long before Colbert's death and Le Brun's subsequent removal from power, disputes began, as in the other arts, between *les Anciens* and *les Modernes,* between 'les Poussinistes' and 'les Rubénistes', the champions of realism and those of colour. The battle was first joined in 1668, when the leader of the *Rubénistes,* Roger de Piles, published his annotation to Dufresnoy's *De Arte Graphica* (where he, in fact, gives more praise to Titian than to Rubens).

In June 1671, Philippe de Champaigne, in a lecture on a picture by Titian, gave his support to the cause of drawing, but a few months later Blanchard answered him with a fiery discourse on the importance of colour (and the heart of the quarrel is very well represented here in Plates 61 and 62, in which Blanchard's Titianesque *Angelica and Médor,* with its yielding contours, diffused light and Venetian colour, is confronted by the severe architecture of Poussin's *Rinaldo and Armida).* Le Brun was asked to intervene in the quarrel, and in February 1672 he gave his verdict in favour of drawing. In the next year, however, Roger de Piles replied with his *Dialogue de Couleur,* in which he went so far to assert that paintings by Rubens were more beautiful than nature, and that drawing was only an adjunct to colouring. The dispute was to continue for twenty years until, in 1695, the Academy at least acknowledged the *Rubéniste* position by electing de Piles an honorary member. By that time not only had

31

the Academy's authority slackened, but the taste for the work of the Dutch and Flemish schools was growing among collectors and connoisseurs as well as artists.

*

THE LAST thirty years of Louis' reign present a striking contrast to the two brilliant and confident decades before 1685. These were not only years of spiritual disillusionment for a king whose life and court were now dominated by the narrow piety of Madame de Maintenon, but a period of religious enmity and military disaster. In 1685, the year of Colbert's death, the revocation of the Edict of Nantes, which had permitted Protestants to practise their religion in freedom, drove from France four hundred thousand of Louis' ablest subjects. By this time also England, the Empire, Holland, Spain and Sweden had come into league against him. The sun had not merely gone behind a cloud, but was indeed sinking below the horizon.

The retirement of Le Brun was only one sign of the revolt against those artistic principles which had ruled French art for half a century, a reaction against the grandiose and the monumental as presented in the language of the Italian and classical traditions. The work at Versailles was completed. The Gobelin factory closed down. Patronage was passing from court and aristocracy to the rich bourgeoisie, who asked, not for allegory or history, but for scenes of contemporary life, for scenes of love and good living.

Among the main precursors of the eighteenth century were the portrait painters Hyacinth Rigaud, whose work showed the influence of Rembrandt, and Nicholas de Largillière. The latter was born in Paris but educated in Antwerp where he worked, until he was eighteen, for a minor Flemish artist named Goebow. He spent the next six years in England as an assistant and drapery painter to Sir Peter Lely, returning at the age of twenty-four to Paris, where he painted until his death in 1746. His portraits, many of which represent groups of prosperous merchants and bourgeois, are in extreme contrast to the work of such painters as Philippe de Champaigne. Their colour and the brilliant painting of the drapery which he had learnt as much from Van Dyck as from any other painter, are immediately decorative. He gave to his sitters some of that animation which was to be so characteristic of the pastel portraits of de la Tour, and which can be seen in the portraits of himself, his wife and his daughter (Plate 70). Here a lively movement flows through every part of the figures, and the gestures of their hands and arms give a natural vitality to the poses. The silks, satins and lace of their clothes have acquired some of that sparkling texture which shines out from so many eighteenth-century canvases.

Charles Desportes represents another aspect of that northern influence which was shaping the art of the new century. His self-portrait with his gun, his dogs and the pile of dead game (Plate 72), a conception which follows so closely the work of a Flemish painter like Snyders, is an appropriate symbol of his activities. He was 'Peintre de la Chasse' to Louis XIV, and after service as a court painter in Poland and a visit to England, he designed a famous series of eight hunting scenes for the Gobelin tapestries. An even more distinguished painter in this field, who was to work for Louis XV as Desportes had for his predecessor, was Jean-Baptiste Oudry. Oudry made a splendid set of illustrations to the fables of La Fontaine, and became chief inspector of the Gobelin works. The Still Life (Plate 71) is among his finest achievements, though a comparison with almost any Chardin will quickly reduce its effect to the level of a superb piece of decorative and technical virtuosity. For all its apparent originality, it does not carry the art of painting forward as Chardin did in his more modest picture of a pile of peaches, for example (Plate 83a).

Louis XIV died in 1715 and the rule passed for eight years into the hands of a regent, Philippe d'Orléans, whose personality and policy fulfilled the desire of French society to be emancipated from the severities and disillusionment of the preceding twenty years. Philippe helped to create a new Paris, no longer just the political capital of the nation as it had been when the court was at Versailles, but a city devoted to social pleasures and intellectual pursuits, that city which has entertained and enlightened Europe ever since. The theatre and the opera assumed a new importance. The Italian comedians, banished from the country by Louis XIV, returned under their famous leader, Riccoboni. Masked balls were held in the Opéra and the Tuileries Gardens, and many new hotels, less grandiose than those of a century before, were built, their walls inviting decorations which would reflect the new taste.

The ideal painter-laureate for such a society was at hand: Antoine Watteau. Watteau, who was born in Valenciennes in 1684, was by origin not French but Flemish. He was the son of an artisan, and the earliest paintings to survive show his debt to such Dutch artists as Teniers. After two years of hack work in Paris, he joined the studio of Claude Gillot, an artist of very limited powers, but one whose interests and enthusiasms were to have an important influence upon Watteau's art. Gillot enjoyed making spontaneous records of the passing show and particularly the life of the theatre. All these drawings display a minor wit and elegance, and there is no doubt that one of the habits which were to guide Watteau's painting—his accumulation of drawings—is largely due to his apprenticeship with Gillot. After five years he moved to the studio of Claude III Audran, an interior decorator whose 'grotesques' and 'arabesques' also helped to form the young artist's calligraphy. More important, however, was the fact that Audran was the keeper of the Luxembourg Palace and thus in charge of those Rubens panels of the Life of Marie de Medici, which were to be for many French artists of the eighteenth and nineteenth centuries what Masaccio's Brancacci Chapel frescoes had been to Italian painters of the fifteenth and sixteenth centuries.

Watteau's knowledge of earlier masters was to be strengthened still further when, in 1704, the art dealer Sirois introduced him to the banker, Pierre Crozat; and on two occasions Watteau went to live in Crozat's mansion as the curator of his splendid collections. The famous banker owned those works formerly belonging to Jabach which had not been bought by Colbert for Louis XIV, and besides some five hundred pictures, he possessed nineteen thousand drawings including many by Rubens and the Venetian masters—in particular, Titian and Veronese—upon whose vision and technique Watteau's painting was to be so firmly and yet so independently built.

This is one of the most extraordinary transformations in the history of art. Veronese, Titian, Rubens were all confident extroverts celebrating the richness of life with little hint of doubt and no hint at all of mortality, with no suggestion that life may be frail and shortlived. Watteau, having paid due attention to these exuberant paintings, proceeded to create a fragile world inhabited by Harlequin and Columbine, by lovers lost in the temporary enjoyment of each other's company, encounters of musicians and actors, or small solitary figures slipping gracefully but without assurance through those idyllic groves which he had found in the grounds of the Luxembourg Palace or in the drawings of Campagnola. But it is impossible

3

to say what indeed is occurring in any of these pictures, for they suggest happenings more profound than any represented by the actions of the figures. This world of subtle implications, of transient encounters, might well have been merely a fanciful charade, however profoundly in many of its details and in its spirit it served as a true symbol of the Regency. What gives these paintings their profound and imaginative reality, however, is the essential truth of every figure and every action, the turn of a head, the pointing of a toe, the flutter of slight fingers over the strings of a guitar, the meeting of hands and the shimmer of light on a silk dress, the suave gestures of a courtly *galante* or the activity of a flea-hunting dog. The source of this visual truth lay behind the paintings, in those wonderful drawings in chalk—red, black and white—which Watteau kept in a bound volume as his pictorial dictionary. For his paintings are a synthesis, most carefully achieved, of a host of visual experiences of other people's pictures, of familiar buildings and landscapes, of the friends who have posed for him. The drawings are still alive with the gestures which laid the marks upon the paper, and the tiny, delicate touches of broken colour which contain the shifting light on skin and drapery and foliage have a similar immediacy. Even a more prosaic subject, the signboard which he painted for his friend Gersaint, the art-dealer, has this peculiar ambiguity (Plates 77–78).

Watteau died of consumption in 1721, but his example was to exert its influence throughout the century, as much through the engravings published after his death and the work of his immediate followers, Lancret and Pater, as through his own paintings. Lancret was with Watteau in Gillot's studio, and comparison of Plate 73 with the wonderful *Embarkation for Cythera* on the opposite page is enough to show that his derivations from Watteau carried with them no implications or undertones. They were sensitive statements of fact, hardly biased by imagination or temperament.

For all its deficiencies, the Regency had transformed French life and French culture, setting the pattern for the reign of Louis XV which followed. In spite of the country's defeat in wars abroad, the next fifty years were to be a time of prosperity, a prosperity recorded so aptly by the gilded and ornate furniture, the rich draperies, the silver and the porcelain, which with the decorations of a Boucher made the houses of the aristocracy and the new rich middle-class into palaces. This was a period also of intense intellectual energy and of respect for that intellectual freedom and restraint which the *philosophes* found in English institutions and sought to bring into their own society. Elegance rather than grandeur, wit and intelligence rather than doctrinaire opinion, realism rather than rationalism: these were the characteristics of French eighteenth-century culture. An art which flattered, which sought to give immediate sensual pleasure or which referred to what was enjoyable in daily living; such an art found its appropriate form in the Rococo, with its elegance, its light serpentine forms and its lack of any structural discipline.

If Watteau had been the typical and emblematic painter of the Regency, Boucher expressed the feeling of the next fifty years. Boucher was not only a sensualist, but a man of strenuous intellectual energy who almost matched Charles Le Brun in the variety of his talents and the scale of his ambition. Apart from his enormous production of paintings and drawings—he was the first artist to exhibit drawings (in the two-yearly Salons)—he acted as director of the Gobelins between 1755 and 1770, as successor to Oudry, and made designs not only for that factory, but at least forty for the one at Beauvais. He was, besides, '*Premier Peintre du Roi*', director of the Academy and the favourite painter of Madame de Pompadour, that remarkable woman whose extremely influential patronage of the arts arose not only from her natural taste and enthusiasms, but also from an awareness of its political value.

Although the early doctrines of the Academy had suffered some modification after the death of Le Brun, although the *Rubénistes'* reaction had permitted a Watteau and, later, a Chardin to become members of the Academy, the grand manner of history painting, with its changing but restricted formulæ, persisted throughout the century, and it was only by its standards that the status and achievement of painters continued to be judged. It was to the history painters that the prizes and the best commissions went.

\*

CHARDIN, a lifelong inhabitant of Paris, was the son of a master carpenter, who, appropriately enough for a craftsman, made him a member of that ancient Guild of St. Luke which had guarded the standards of painting long before the existence of the Academy. He was apprenticed to two minor artists: first to René-Jacques Cazes and then to Noël-Nicolas Coypel, one of a family which raised painters for nearly two hundred years. It was not until he had been working for fifteen years that he achieved any success, and then, in 1728, he exhibited two pictures, *La Raie* and *Le Buffet*. The first of these paintings was bought by the academician Van Loo (who is represented in Plate 84), and much admired by de Largillière of the Academy. In the following year Chardin became a full member as a *"peintre des fleurs, fruits et de genre"*.

Chardin continued to develop his art slowly, and during the next few years he painted a group of those '*Singeries*'—studies of monkeys in human clothing, a type of picture which dated back to the middle of the previous century, and had become most popular during the Regency. Then in 1732, he exhibited *Sealing the Letter*, the first of that great series of pictures depicting people engaged in everyday tasks: cooks, maidservants, washerwomen, and mothers looking after their children. During the next ten years he exhibited thirty-one paintings of this character (Plates 81–82) and then for the last thirty-seven years of his life devoted himself, apart from a number of pastel portraits, to the painting of still life. The change in taste which had come about since the day of Louis XIV and Le Brun is most strikingly obvious in the public attitude to Chardin, whose pictures stood low in that hierarchy of the art established by the Academy, and whose most obvious predecessors, the brothers Le Nain, had passed almost unnoticed. Although Chardin never made a fortune from his work and, indeed, was glad of the support of the pension he received in 1734 and for his salary as treasurer to the Academy (a post he received in the following year), although the kind of pictures he painted could only command a small price, he was a highly regarded, even a popular artist. His pictures were bought and commissioned not only by Louis XV but by collectors all over Europe. Engravings after his pictures were sold in great numbers in England and Germany as well as in France. He was widely praised by writers and critics, no doubt for qualities which would today seem incidental to his real achievements; for his most obvious quality, realism, for the resemblance which his work bore to Flemish art, and in the case of that most influential critic, Denis Diderot who required a painting to record a moral precept, for his faithfulness to appearances and the virtuous domesticity of his subjects.

Chardin's modest financial success was partly due to the slowness with which he worked, and appropriate to that is the extremely narrow range of his subject matter. Besides, he made many replicas of earlier paintings. Nearly all those features which are characteristic of the other artists of the period are absent from Chardin's art. He never painted the nude, nor scenes of love or gallantry; he avoided mythology and history, and disguised his few portraits of actual people by giving them other titles. He avoided all the textures most common in eighteenth-century pictures: silk, satin, precious stones, fur (except on a dead animal), polished marble, porcelain, silver and gold. Instead, his textures are rough cloth and coarse linen, pottery, copper, steel, the bloom on fruit and dusty surfaces. His still lifes, after those early, ambitious pictures like *La Raie*, would not excite the appetite either of the gourmet or the gourmand. His maidservants suggest no subtle or hidden beauty; indeed the faces of his people offer no greater variety of expression than Cézanne's, and perform only a simple repertoire of gestures. Chardin was a man with a box of colours, working very close to the abstract principles of painting; working out with the bare necessities of life, food, cooking utensils, and the simplest of human activities, principles of volume, scale and interval, the relationships between light and texture.

Cézanne once said, "I think I could be occupied for months without changing my place, simply bending a little more to the right or left." The same words might be applied to Chardin. He abstracted from the academic field of history painting that pictorial science which Poussin had mastered, and applied it so magnificently to humble objects that they acquired the grandeur of an epic.

\*

The eighteenth century saw something of a revival of the demand for portraiture which had been so characteristic of the sixteenth century, and there was a particular fashion for pastel portraits, a fashion formed at the time of the Regency, when the Venetian artist, Rosalba Carriera, visited Paris. The two finest practitioners of this art were Maurice-Quentin de la Tour and Jean-Baptiste Perronneau. La Tour was a brilliantly skilful portraitist. His paintings give one the immediate impression of being vividly like the sitter, and they are always presented with an almost overpowering physical realism. Indeed, his people are generally endowed with such a vivacity that they seem to be leaning forward, out of the picture's frame. La Tour was a character independent, argumentative and no respecter of persons, even when his sitters were royalty. His eccentricities multiplied rather than diminished his patronage and, in this respect, he was unlike Perroneau, who was not only of a reserved temperament, but failed to achieve his rival's popularity.

La Tour's technique is brilliant and assured and the attitude of his people vigorous; Perronneau's handling is delicate and reserved, his figures have a quiet liveliness, their expressions are elusive and withdrawn. At his best Perroneau's portraits show some of Gainsborough's silvery tonality and melting paint. The portraiture of a later generation is represented here by Duplessis, who exhibits all that sympathy and charm which is to be expected of the period, but with it a more emphatic realism which looks forward to the portraiture of David.

Watteau, Boucher, Fragonard; these names span the century from the reign of Louis XIV to the Revolution. Fragonard was born in 1732; he worked with Boucher, won the *Prix de Rome* and spent four years in Italy. On his return in 1761, the history picture which had grown out of this training, *Le Grand Prêtre Corésus se sacrifie pour sauver Callirhoé,* brought him election to the Academy. When the money for this picture, which had been bought for the Gobelins, was slow in coming, he began to paint those small paintings of lovers by which he is best known. It was at this time too that he began to receive many commissions to decorate the apartments of the demi-monde, and became a familiar figure in that extravagant and licentious society which revolved about such notorious figures as the dancer La Guimard, one of his patrons. At this period also, he made that series of decorations (which were never to be put up) for Madame du Barry's Pavillon de Louveciennes. From this time forward Fragonard ceased to exhibit in the *Salons* and sold his pictures direct from his studio.

In the history of French art Poussin and Cézanne can be taken to represent the extreme of self-discipline, Fragonard the other extreme of self-indulgence and uncontrolled sensation. There was very little that he did not paint, except—not surprisingly—that kind of picture which David's dictatorship was to impose upon the taste of Revolutionary society during the last years of Fragonard's life. He painted all the gaiety and extravagance of eighteenth-century Paris; picturesque landscapes, idyllic scenes of country life, portraits and those domestic incidents upon which his contemporary, Greuze, was to turn his sentimental and moralising attention. He was equally adept at adopting styles and mannerisms and fitting them to his purpose. In Plate 90 he has transformed a Boucher into something so flippant and yet at the same time so vividly realistic that what results is almost a parody of Boucher, of the period and of himself. How he was influenced by the dramatic lighting of Rembrandt, and how he used that example to a slight picturesque effect, is shown in Plate 88.

He was a painter whose feelings lay very close to the point of his brush, a brush invariably fluent and dexterous. He had an uncanny gift for recording texture (Plates 88 and 90), and a marked sense of drama—of drama without passion or character but one which can endow the most trivial conception with a temporary magic. His art is without any of that profound seriousness which alone makes triviality bearable.

Fragonard's friend, Hubert Robert, who was with him in Italy, seems to have been equally fluent, for Madame Vigé Lebrun said of him that he painted a picture as quickly as he wrote a letter. Robert had worked in Rome with Claude's pupil, Pannini, and he was much affected by the excavations at Herculaneum, an early landmark in the history of classical archæology.

After his return to Paris, he became, in 1770, '*Dessinateur des Jardins du Roi*'. His painting of the *Pont du Gard* (Plate 91), the most magnificent of all the Roman remains of Provence, displays not only his perception of the romantic possibilities of architecture, but also that profound appreciation of the particular character of architectural style and of the relation of architecture to landscape which makes him the greatest master of the eighteenth-century Picturesque.

The Rococo had not destroyed history painting even if it had banished much of the high seriousness of its seventeenth-century character, and by the middle of the century a neo-classical revival was in train. This was stimulated in turn by the dilettante's interest in classical monuments and by the publication of such influential works as Stuart and Revett's *Antiquities of Athens* and, above all, Winckelmann's *Geschichte der Kunst*, one of the gospels of neo-classicism in Europe. Almost as powerful in France was the influence of the Comte de Caylus, who published the finds at Pompeii and patronised such artists as David's master, Vien, and who, in spite of his own very moderate talent, could at least claim thereby to have had some influence upon the art of the Revolutionary period.

THE REVOLUTION brought with it changes in the organisation of the arts. In 1793, the *Académie Royale* was abolished, and in its place the Revolutionary Government established a *Commune Générale des Arts.* Private patronage had now virtually come to an end, and the Commune was to employ artists, among other means, by instituting competitions for pictures which glorified the nation and the new *régime*.

A *Musée Nationale des Arts* was founded to take charge of works of art from royal palaces, churches and from the private collections of *émigrés*, which had been seized as national property. Money was also made available for the purchase of masterpieces which might otherwise have been sold out of the country. The *Académie Royale* was succeeded in 1795 by the *Institut National*, which included the section later to be known as the *Académie des Beaux-Arts*.

The leader of this activity was the painter Jacques-Louis David, who in 1792, at the age of forty-four, became a deputy in the Convention; for two years he was controller of the artistic policy of the new republic, designer of revolutionary fêtes and processions, and commemorator of such contemporary martyrs as Marat and Barra. In 1794, after the fall of Robespierre, he himself became a suspect, and was twice imprisoned in the Luxembourg Palace. On his final release he abandoned politics and was given a studio by the directorate, where he painted his *Rape of the Sabines*.

When Napoleon became Emperor, David was appointed 'Premier Peintre de L'Empéreur', and was commissioned to make a series of pictures of the great imperial ceremonies, of which the finest are *Le Sacre de Napoleon I* and *Le Serment de L'Armée après la Distribution des Aigles*. If Roman subjects and costumes had given way to the brilliance of imperial pageantry, the design of these two vast compositions was still strictly controlled by David's neo-classical principles. But in spite of these paintings, and of his loyalty to the new government, David could not regain the control of artistic affairs which he had exercised in the first years of the Revolution; so, retiring again from political life, he returned to the painting of *Leonidas before Thermopylae* which he had begun in 1880, and in which the figure of Leonidas was derived from an illustration in Winckelmann's *Monuments Inédits*. During the Hundred Days, Napoleon visited the painter's studio to see this picture, and it was for his support of the Emperor at this time that David was exiled in 1816 by Louis XVIII. Until his death in 1825 he lived in Brussels.

As a young man, David had been advised by Boucher to adopt Vien as his teacher; when, in 1774, David gained the *Prix de Rome* at the fifth attempt, Vien, recently appointed Director of the Academy in Rome, accompanied him to that city. David had once been sufficiently sympathetic towards the contemporary current of taste and artistic practice to finish a commission for Fragonard, but three years in Rome transformed him into a doctrinaire rebel with a determination to revive the æsthetics of Poussin. *Le Serment des Horaces* (Plate 93) was, in fact, designed to be a deliberate challenge to the Rococo, a reassertion of classical values and forms. This picture, *The Death of Socrates* shown at the *Salon* in 1787 and the *Brutus* exhibited there after the Revolution had begun in 1789, were not only the development of that æsthetic intention, but of David's desire to make an art which would be useful—a means of enlightening his fellow citizens and of "putting before their eyes the noble aspect of heroism and virtue". Indeed, the *Brutus* was regarded by many, in the violent year of its first appearance, as a militant sermon on behalf of those republican virtues which had also existed in Roman society.

There are those who may find it hard to reconcile the harsh realism of the *Marat Assassiné* (Plate 92) or the more benign realism of such portraits as those of *Madame Récamier*, or *Madame Chalgrin* (Plates 94-95), with the severe classicism of those history pictures which most completely represent David's intentions, with their hard, sculptural modelling and dry, cold colour, their formal design and rigid gestures. Confronted by such an uncompromising art it is easy to lose sight of the realism of so much of its detail, that kind of realism indeed which makes the figure of Marat, poised between the two superbly realised planes of the wall and the box, one of the most powerful images in French art. And so it has always been easy to compare David's work unfavourably with the more hot-blooded and libertarian painting which was to follow, with that of Géricault or Delacroix. It is easy to forget the insight of David's splendid portraits and that commanding realism which lives among the togas, the Roman armour and the imperial eagles. The hand of the father in *Le Serment des Horaces* is no less humanly eloquent than the quivering hand of the sailor thrown against the sky in Géricault's *The Raft of the Medusa* (Plate 98), or the tense arm of Delacroix' figure of Liberty (Plate 107).

The greatest of David's pupils was Ingres, who entered his studio in 1796 at the age of sixteen, keeping himself by playing the violin in a boulevard theatre. Having won the *Prix de Rome* he could not afford to go to that city until 1806, and it was in the interval that he painted the splendid portraits of the Rivières, husband, wife and daughter (Plate 102).

Ingres remained in Rome until 1820, and there he discovered and copied the works of his favourite master, Raphael. For him, Raphael was more than the greatest of painters—"il était beau, il était bon, il était tout". After Rome, Florence, where he stayed for four years before returning to Paris in 1844. The paintings he sent from Italy to the *Salon* were consistently attacked by those critics who supported the Davidian ideal. For them *The Jupiter et Thétis*, which was in the *Salon* in 1811, and *La Grande Odalisque* (Plate 103), exhibited three years later, were a betrayal of David's classical integrity. According to such critics they broke all his rules of proportion, they marked, in fact, a return to a Gothic crudity and eccentricity.

Back in Paris, Ingres briefly acknowledged the new taste for mediævalism and romantic history pieces by painting a number of pictures which represented scenes from French history and literature; but this interlude did not last long, and with the *Apotheosis of Homer* of 1827 he reasserted his position as the leader of the classical school, a position he was to hold both in Paris and in Rome (whither he returned in 1834 to be Director of the Academy).

Ingres' critics were at least right to find him a radical deviation from the principles which he might have learnt from David. The subtle refinement of his drawing, the infinitely smooth modulation from plane to plane which is so characteristic of his modelling, and his attention to detail, may easily blind us to those distortions essential to his method; those distortions which rule the mannerist rhythms of his *Grande Odalisque*. For, if David was a doctrinaire convinced of the need to provide, through painting, ennobling and socially useful truth, Ingres was equally a doctrinaire, but in pursuit of ideal beauty. "*Il n'y a pas des arts*", he wrote, "*il n'y en a pas, il n'y en a qu'un; c'est celui qui a pour fondement le beau éternel et naturel.*" Elsewhere, "*N'étudiez le beau qu'à genoux*". If David was a Roman, Ingres was a Greek. Drawing was for him "*La probité de l'art*"; indeed it was through drawing more than any other means of expression that beauty could be achieved, and that, by means of lines which were to be in themselves beautiful; beautiful with a refined, rhythmical simplicity. Such simple lines meant simple, ideal forms, and such ideal forms could only exist where the paint was kept to an enamel smoothness, and colour restrained to a tint. The distortions in the *Grande Odalisque* arise from Ingres' search for the beautiful contour and the simple form. For him the ideal was not represented, as it had been for David or the history painters of the seventeenth century, by an acceptance of classical proportions, but by following one's own instinct for what is beautiful. The progressive movements of the century, from Delacroix to Cézanne were, as we shall see, to offer a funda-mental repudiation of this ideal.

Apart from the drawings and some of the early figure pictures, it is Ingres' portraits which do most to sustain his reputation, for there that dangerous quest for an ideal beauty can operate least powerfully. There are few finer portraits in French art than that of *Monsieur Bertin* (Plate 101), painted in 1832, a portrait embodying indeed a whole history not only of the sitter but of the bourgeois society which he represents. As a contrast to the stubborn and self-assertive angularity of M. Bertin we have the portrait of *Mademoiselle Rivière* (Plate 102), with its complex counterpoint of curves echoing the rounded top of the canvas, and the exquisite subtlety of contours and modelling. This picture shows what beauty Ingres could achieve when he was diverted a little from his ideal by the claims of a commission.

\*

WHEN IN 1800 David was painting Madame Récamier reclining on that couch which he himself had designed ten years before, his sitter was tempted by the slowness of his progress and the advice of her friends to patronise another painter. This was one of David's pupils, François Gérard, who is known now not so much for his historical compositions as for such portraits as Plate 100, in which he combined with the Davidian ideal of form much of that easy elegance and sweetness which had been so general before the Revolution. Apart from Ingres, the most definite personality among David's following was Baron le Gros, who was attached to Napoleon's staff, painting not only many portraits of the Emperor, but large pictures of his battles and other triumphs. Gros, who committed suicide in 1834, had very little of David's austerity and was, indeed, of a profoundly romantic temperament. The extent to which this led him to anticipate the work of Géricault is seen in his *Les Pestiférés de Jaffa* (Plate 97), an incident from Napoleon's Egyptian campaigns. The figure holding the basket of bread might indeed be one of David's centurions, but two of the main sufferers in the centre of the canvas might equally have escaped from *The Raft of the Medusa,* while the oriental architecture and landscape constitute a not quite formal setting—they are painted with some of that excitement for the east which painters were to be expressing so consistently a few years later. Gros' painting is divided between the conventions he had acquired in his master's studio and that new realism which was about to challenge the Davidian authority.

The history of French art from the Revolution to the end of the nineteenth century is punctuated by a succession of paintings, some of which were to cause public controversy and scandal, all of which were consciously or unconsciously to be the manifestoes of a new direction in painting. David's *Brutus* and *Marat Assassiné* and Ingres' *Jupiter et Thétis* have already been mentioned. Delacroix' *Scènes des Massacres de Scio* (Plate 106), Courbet's *Enterrement à Ornans,* Manet's *Le Déjeuner sur l'Herbe* (Plate 119), Degas' *Vicomte Lepic* and Seurat's *Une Baignade— Asnières* (Plate 138) were to follow. To this list must, however, be added, Géricault's *Le Radeau de la Méduse* (Plate 98), exhibited at the *Salon* in 1819. Géricault was then twenty-eight, and he had only five more years to live. He was born at Rouen, the son of wealthy middle-class parents. When the family moved to Paris he worked first in the studio of the animal painter Carle Vernet and then with another of David's pupils, Pierre Guérin, who said of his work that it resembled nature as much as a violin case resembled a violin.

Géricault's personality presents a curious tension of passion and order. He was a devoted horseman, indeed, pictures of horses, generally in violent action, make up the larger part of his work. His early death was to follow a riding mishap. Had he lived, he might well have fought at the Barricades in 1830 and 1848; as it was, he enrolled for a brief period during the Hundred Days in the *mousquetaires*. Not long afterward, following some emotional crisis, he went to Italy, where he studied the Michelangelos and painted a series of pictures of the annual horse race on the Corso in which the extreme violence of the animals' movements is ordered into a classical frieze.

It was on his return from Rome that he began work on the *Medusa,* a frigate wrecked on a voyage to Senegal; of the 149 souls who had crowded the raft when the ship had sunk, only fifteen remained to be rescued, twelve days later. This picture was to be a modern history piece of a significant kind. Its subject was not one preselected by patronage, public taste or national fervour. It did not celebrate any military event or the might or justice of the *régime* (in fact the incident had caused some criticism of the administration). It did not recreate some fashion-able myth or historical action, nor celebrate a hero. Its subject was not attractive. It was a museum picture, but, what was more important, it gave Géricault an opportunity to exercise his personal interests—his interest in anatomy, in human psychology and in the drama of human conflict. It may be linked on one hand to Ford Madox Brown's *The Last of England,* and on the other to Manet's *Execution of the Emperor Maximilian.* Géricault approached the task with characteristic energy and thoroughness. Not only did he question all available witnesses, but he had made a model of the raft. He studied human suffering in the Hôpital Beaujon, and his studio became filled with anatomical specimens. Here was realism not for the sake of any ideal but pursued in his own interests.

This picture, which caused such excitement at the *Salon* and so much unfavourable criticism from the school of David, was, later in 1820, exhibited in England, where Géricault lived for two years. Among Géricault's last works are a group of six magnificent portraits (Plates 99 and 99a) of insane people, which throw a revealing light upon his pictorial realism and upon his temperament. They were commissioned by a Dr. Georget, who occupies an important place in the history of mental therapy. At this period the treatment of the insane was undergoing a revolution. Instead of regarding them as evil creatures, fit only for imprison-ment or at best a raree-show, as had been the case in the past, Georget and others treated their patients as human beings with a separate life and world of their own, which must be studied and ministered to with care and respect. This is also the spirit of these magnificent portraits. Géricault has not devised gross caricatures for these different *'folies'* but has recorded their features with a wonderfully sympathetic detachment. They provide an answer to those who find in his art a sinister morbidity and a perverse attachment to violence.

In 1824, the year of Géricault's death, Eugène Delacroix, who had worked with him in Guérin's studio, exhibited at the *Salon* his *Massacres de Scio* (Plate 106), also inspired by contemporary events—an incident in those wars of Greek Independence in which Byron had fought and died. It is well known that Delacroix largely revised this picture under the influence of the fresh colour and spontaneous handling of Constable's *Hay Wain,* which was shown in Paris that year. An even more profound influence, however, had already been at work upon the shaping of Delacroix' art—the discovery of Rubens, whose panels depicting the life of Marie de Medici had been brought to the Louvre from the Luxembourg Palace in 1818, to fill the gaps left when Napoleon's plunder was returned to its owners. In 1822 Delacroix' *Dante et Virgile* had been shown with much comment at the *Salon,* and by 1831 he had added to this list of portentous works *La Mort de Sardanapale* and *Le 28 Juillet 1830: La Liberté guidant le Peuple* (Plate 107), which was bought by Louis Philippe. These paintings had made Delacroix famous, and generally unpopular among the supporters of the *Institut des Beaux-Arts.*

In 1832 he went to Morocco with the French Ambassador to the Sultan—that visit which he describes so brilliantly in his journal—and in the following year, to Spain. There followed a succession of oriental subjects which were to exercise an immediate and considerable influence. It was during the next fifteen years that he worked that series of decorative schemes which gave full scope to his genius such as the designs for the Luxembourg, the Palais Bourbon and the Hôtel de Ville. He died in 1863, only six years after his belated election to the *Institut.*

One may find in Delacroix' art all those themes which are so characteristic of what is loosely called the Romantic Movement: those scenes of violent physical action and emotional conflict, as in the Scio painting; the employment of the horse or the savage animal as the embodiment of terror, violence, liberty or captivity; the struggle for human liberty against restraint (as in *La Liberté guidant le Peuple);* moments of psychological drama often to be extracted from Dante, from the plays of Shakespeare, the poetry of Byron or the novels of Walter Scott; mediævalism and orientalism.

For Delacroix, a man of great intelligence, these themes were not employed solely for a picturesque purpose, but because they expressed so often and in so many ways the principle of vitality, of grandeur and of dignity in Man. And so the subjects he depicted were liberated from that pedantry or undue attention to historical or documentary accuracy which had destroyed so much academic painting. Indeed, an academic conference of the seventeenth century would have found everything to criticise in this respect. Delacroix' scenes from the Bible or from literature (see the *Tobias and the Angel*—Plate 108) escape from the pages of the book and receive a new life. Delacroix' Moroccans are not people to be regarded with curiosity or with a nostalgia for the primitive, but as the vital representatives of a dignified race. His animals do not lose their identity and become a mirror for human emotions.

It is important, however, to penetrate even deeper into Delacroix' artistic personality if his influence upon the nineteenth century is to be understood, for perhaps even more important was his reinterpretation of the combined traditions of Venetian painting and the art of Rubens, which he projected as a guide and an inspiration to those masters of the last half of the century, who so often acknowledge the debt. Cézanne planned, though he never completed, an *Apotheosis of Delacroix* in which the figures of Pissarro and Monet as well as himself were to appear. Corot, Daumier, Manet, Renoir, Degas and, in particular Van Gogh, were others who expressed their reverence for him. His æsthetic is the source of all that is most valuable and creative in the French painting of the last half of the century. Delacroix was passionately responsive to the appearance of things, not only the movements of the human body and the splendid colours which he discovered in Morocco, but such slight discoveries as the pattern made by rippling water in the mud at the bottom of a pond. But he was never seduced by such observations, as were many artists of this naturalist century. For he found the most real things to be those images which he created in his paintings; as truth, he believed, depends upon the artist and not upon any system which lies outside his personality. He demanded the rule of the imagination, but imagination controlled by reason and by that taste which is 'spiritual lucidity'.

In his drawing he challenged the conception of the beautiful line which ruled the art of Ingres and the *Institut,* and substituted a drawing in which the form was created by the right accumulation of strokes having no individual value other than vitality. He not only brought back into painting the rich palette of Rubens and the Venetians, as can be seen in his splendid *Still Life* (Plate 107a), and challenged once again the *Poussiniste* æsthetic of so many of his contemporaries; but he himself advanced the study of colour, by showing, or rather reviving, the knowledge that shadows are not colourless and cannot be truly expressed by a deepening of the tone. The art of the Impressionist finds its herald in this painter whom Van Gogh described as the pioneer of modern painting.

✳

THE MIDDLE years of the century saw the emergence of a school of *'paysagistes',* who combined the modest vision of the Dutch landscape painters of the seventeenth century with something of Constable's atmospheric realism. Nevertheless, these painters of the Barbizon School, such as Rousseau, Daubigny and Dupré, had little of the sturdiness of the Dutch or the temperamental fire of Constable. They did not push their observation of nature to the point where it engaged their emotions, nor did the fundamental simplicity and directness of their vision work with the ardour of a Courbet. They were, indeed, naturalists, and naturalism could represent the worst as well as the best art of the period.

The most considerable artist among this group was Jean-François Millet, the son of a poor Norman peasant family, who went to live at Barbizon in 1848, when he was forty-four. He was not, like Courbet, politically conscious nor a strenuous social propagandist, and yet his pictures of peasant life, such as *L'Angélus* are generally sententious in a way unknown in Courbet's art. For these peasant pictures, whose character is so often derived from Dutch genre painting, are tinged with that kind of nineteenth-century philanthropy which makes their mood particularly unacceptable today. If this overtone, however, can be neglected, Millet assumes the status of a painter of some power and insight, especially in his drawings, or in such pictures as Plate 110, where the subject has nothing to do with the dignity of labour, and where he does achieve a pictorial realism which, at least, gives him a claim to be associated with Courbet. The finest landscape painter of this generation was an independent, Camille Corot. Although his parents would not allow him to be more than a spare-time painter until he was twenty-eight years old, Corot was one of those artists who enjoyed a small private income, which enabled him not only to travel in Italy, but also to paint for many years without selling a picture. Corot was among the least theoretical, the most modest and the most passive of French painters. He devised no symbolism for his sensations. Either, as in his earlier landscapes, he made a faithful record of what he saw or, when observation grew less important, worked to a simple formula. He wrote, "Be guided by feeling alone. We are only simple mortals subject to error . . . Be firm, be meek, but follow your own convictions . . . Beauty in art is truth bathed in an impression received from nature . . . I am struck upon seeing a certain place . . . While I strive for a conscientious imitation, I never for an instant lose the emotion which has taken hold of me."

Such a vague and essentially untheoretical statement is typical of the man. Corot places his reliance upon a precise observation of tone values, to which he was invariably sensitive. His early landscapes are compact and luminous, and give the impression that the painter has interfered hardly at all with his immediate sensations. The landscapes are always bathed in a particular and subtle glow of light, but this luminosity is not the result of any analysis. There is invariably a sense of space, and every object is enveloped in atmosphere; but Corot, in fact, never emphasises the structure of any object within that landscape, nor indeed its spatial intervals. Any monochrome (Plate 115) may seem, as fundamentally it is, a little incoherent. The space which lies behind the grass hillock, between its summit and the nearest house, between that and the cathedral, is not explained. The facets of the boulders do not seem to be securely joined, and the whole composition is peacefully inert because its main motives have not been disposed into a tense pattern within the picture frame.

The same absence of structural logic, the same modesty and tenderness, is found in those figure paintings (Plates 113 and 114) which were so little regarded during the painter's lifetime. After 1850, however, Corot became more ambitious and also less reliant upon his wonderful powers of observation. He first attempted to emulate the vision of Claude, and could recreate neither the poetry of that artist's classicism nor the subtle coherence of his design. In the last years of his life he retreated from nature into those naturalistic conventions which proved so popular and successful.

It was not until 1878, and a few months before Daumier's death at the age of seventy, that an exhibition arranged by some of his friends revealed what very few had realised: that the greatest caricaturist and political draughtsman of the century was also a remarkable painter and sculptor. Daumier had begun his career as a lithographer journalist in 1828, and during his lifetime he made about 4,000 lithographs for such journals as *Caricature* and *Charivari*, satirising and attacking the society and the values of his time, its follies and injustices, and, above all, the arrogant presumption of those, such as the politician and the lawyer, who use their authority to prey upon the common man.

Daumier's paintings were made for himself, most of them in the 1860's and '70's. As might be expected from one who was primarily a draughtsman, accustomed also to working out his ideas in clay, the solidity of simple forms, constructed with a strong, bounding line and a tonality of bold contrasts, is the essence of his painting. His figures are carved into masses as rough as those forms of Michelangelo which still lie half imprisoned within their native marble. A caricaturist seeks to command the casual attention and, like the actor, he must simplify his utterance and exaggerate the normal gestures and accents of life. Into one small frame he must concentrate a whole history; his technique must be as straightforward as the words of a parable. Daumier's paintings, like his drawings and lithographs, are generally concerned with the minor dramas of common life, and he had Balzac's gift for presenting these scenes with a rare psychological insight.

Although he could, when he wished, draw a face in all the complexity of its form and expression, Daumier could equally make his figures speak and reveal their personality when

44

the face was only a smudge of white paper or a featureless shadow upon the picture surface; for he was a master of the significant gesture and posture. The painting of an audience watching *Hamlet* (Plate 111) presents in microcosm the very essence of high drama and those emotions which great tragedy can communicate to the audience, transforming the auditorium into a second stage. The other painting reproduced in this book (Plate 112) shows how Daumier could build out of a trivial incident a design of monumental grandeur, and could make common life an affair of eloquent gestures and portentous decisions.

In 1850, there was exhibited at the *Salon*, another of the century's revolutionary works— *Un Enterrement à Ornans*, by Gustave Courbet. Courbet was then thirty-one years old, and his success in winning a medal at the previous *Salon* had given him the privilege of exhibiting this and eight other pictures, including his *Casseurs de Pierres*, without their submission to the jury. The former picture represented a common burial in his native village, the figures of the clergy, the mourners and the other spectators extending in a long shallow file against the rugged Jura landscape, and presented with as little æsthetic elaboration as are the peasants in a painting by Le Nain; every figure had been painted from life.

The picture, and that of the *Stone Breakers*, was violently attacked. Not only, his critics said, were they incompetently painted, with a deliberate coarseness and vulgarity—"an ignoble and impious caricature" one writer called it—but both pictures were held to be a sign of the artist's socialism; from that date his work became, for his opponents, the symbol of a political philosophy, feared and hated by contemporary authority.

Géricault's *The Raft of the Medusa* could at least shelter under the category of history painting, and, to look further back, Chardin's vision of common life was presented on such a modest scale that it implied no challenge to the grand manner. Courbet's painting, however, did not only assert the value of everyday experiences, but suggested that these were the only significant subjects for art and that it is not the painter's business to be a historian, a mythologist and a poet. "Imagination in art", he said, "consists in painting the most complete expression of an existing thing, but never in imagining or in creating the object itself—as I hold that the artists of one century are fundamentally incompetent to represent the thing of a past or future century—in other words to paint the past or the future."

After 1850, encouraged by his friend Proudhon among others, Courbet became an active, if largely emotional, socialist. In 1870 he refused the *Légion d'Honneur,* and when the Second Empire came to an end in that year he was called upon to assume a position similar to that held by David at the time of the Revolution, being elected 'Président de la Commission des Beaux-Arts' and in the following year, a deputy in the *Assemblée Nationale.*

Courbet was unfortunately involved in the destruction of the Vendôme Column and, after the fall of the Commune, was arrested, imprisoned for six months and ordered to pay the cost of its reconstruction. His inability to do this compelled him to leave the country, and he spent the rest of his life in Switzerland.

Courbet's political opinions and his defiant, overbearing personality; Proudhon's statement that his pictures, together with the writings of Auguste Comte, and Proudhon himself, announced "the end of capitalism and the sovereignty of the producers"; Proudhon's interpretation of *Les Casseurs de Pierres* as "crying vengeance in their rags upon art and society" and *Les Demoiselles au bord de la Seine* (Plate 118) as "Pride, Adultery, Divorce and Suicide, replacing cupids, swarm about them as their compassions . . . that is why they finally appear horrible"—all these factors have little to do with the wonderful virtues of Courbet's art. These derive not at all from such motives but from his passionate pursuit of his æsthetic ideal: "Imagination in art consists in finding the most complete expression of an existing thing", and a painter should paint only what his eye can see of what is both "real and existing". It was Courbet who, more than any other artist, enabled the Impressionists to look at the world without æsthetic prejudice.

Few other artists have come so close to the central, unidealised character of what they were painting. The sea has never before or since been recorded with such a perception of its density and its crude power, and the plainness of Courbet's technique always finds the appropriate means to reinforce his vision. Although he is a realist who denied the claims of poetry, his art is in the best sense romantic, a romanticism which the contemporary painter, de Chirico, has found more moving than Delacroix'. "Courbet's romanticism is much more poetic and lonely", de Chirico has written. "Courbet stressed the reality of a figure or an object in the warm light of a summer evening, which he expressed with such great pathos. And this was always the case, whether he painted a figure or a nude, a tree or a rock, or the foamy wave of a stormy sea. But behind the fruit or the leaves one can perceive, far off, the sky and the flying clouds; and behind the women in repose there are windows dividing the trees and the plants of the park into right angles; and behind the rock washed smooth by the sweep of the waves, we see the horizon lit up by the sunset, while the vast skirts of the tempest trail low over the sea. Baudelaire's beautiful lines come to mind,

> Homme libre, toujours tu désiras la mer
> La mer est ton miroir; tu contemples ton âme
> Dans le déroulement infini de sa lame."

\*

"IMPRESSIONISM" may easily become a word as elusive and imprecise as "romanticism", and it would perhaps now be unwise to think of it as anything more than the roughest label for those artists who sent their work to the exhibitions of the Impressionist Group in the '70's and '80's. For any catalogue of impressionist characteristics must contain entries which would not be appropriate to the greatest of those artists.

Certain fundamental conceptions may, however, be suggested which all these artists share. They all employed the common world of everyday experience as a sufficient source for art. They did not create, but found the subjects of their pictures, and benefited accordingly from Courbet's gesture of independence. They maintained a general belief in the value of a strictly optical experience, their art being perceptual rather than conceptual. Finally they felt free to employ the resources of painting to invert techniques, if necessary without loyalty to any academic principles of drawing, colour or composition. And so, if they were indebted to Courbet for the first of these freedoms, it was to Delacroix that they owed this last liberty of expression.

The group came together in 1874 as a gesture of defiance to the *Salon* which had so frequently rejected their work or given it an unsatisfactory display; though Manet, who had suffered most of all, was not a contributor to the first of the exhibitions of that year. The group's thirty members included Boudin, Pissarro, Monet, Sisley, Renoir, Degas and Cézanne. It was a painting by Monet, and its title *Impression—Soleil Levant*, which encouraged a journalist, Louis Leroy, to coin the word "Impressionist". Seven exhibitions were to be held between 1876 and 1886, by which time the impressionist battle had been largely won, and a new generation of artistic experiment was arising to challenge and provoke.

Manet was the son of a rich magistrate who opposed his desire to be a painter, and it was not until 1851 that he was able to begin his training—in the school of Thomas Couture. In 1859, the *Salon* made the first of many rejections of his work, but although his one-man show of that same year (in which the famous portrait of Lola de Valence was included) was generally attacked by the critics, its reception was mild compared with the outcry which greeted *Le Déjeuner sur l'Herbe* (Plate 119). This painting was exhibited in the same year at the *Salon des Refusés*, an exhibition instituted by the Emperor for works rejected from the *Salon*. Based upon an engraving by Marc Antonio, it showed two young men in students' clothes picnicking in a wood with two girls in the nude. It was considered indecent for much the same reasons that had motivated the attacks upon Courbet, for representing without idealism, in terms of modern life and in a technique which enhanced the realism of the scene, a subject which would have been readily accepted if the men had been wearing fancy dress.

Two years later the same assault was made upon his *Olympia* (Plate 122). These attacks drove Manet into a state of persecution mania, and it was in order to escape it all that he visited Madrid, where he came for the first time into contact with those Spanish masters—Velasquez in particular—whose luminous painting, with its emphasis upon exactitude of tone, was to be so decisive in directing Manet's work.

The pictures he exhibited in the years after his return from Spain were all to be ridiculed by critical as well as popular opinion, though he was to find some champions, among them the young novelist Émile Zola, who admired the informal realism of their subjects probably without appreciating their technical innovations. It was only *Le Bon Bock*, exhibited in 1872, which won Manet any praise; and that no doubt only because it could be accepted by eyes attuned to the work of Hals. In 1876 he exhibited at the Second Impressionist Exhibition; while in 1881, two years before his death and twenty years after he had sent his first picture to the *Salon*, he was awarded a medal and the Legion of Honour—and the freedom to hang the works he wished to show.

If, like Courbet, he was attacked for his realism, Manet was equally criticised for the novelty of his technique—particularly in such a picture as Plate 123, where he abandons studio lighting and impenetrable, bituminous shadows, and reduces tone values to their simplest terms of pure, resonant colours, juxtaposed without any modulation. In the heat of their irritation, his critics forgot that many of his innovations were only a rational expansion of practices long accessible in the painting of Velasquez, Goya, or Hals.

The simplicity of his method can be seen in the head of *Olympia* where the minimum of shadow—quick strokes of a luminous grey along the nose and under the chin—has been worked into a general flesh tone sufficient in itself for the expression of the form. This is direct painting without any glazes, and always reveals the artist's gestures (he once wrote to Antoine Proust about his portrait, "I remember as if it were yesterday the quick and summary manner in which I treated the glove in the ungloved hand. And when at that instant you said to me, 'Please, not a line more', I felt that we were in such perfect accord that I could not resist the impulse to embrace you"). These words suggest how devoted Manet was to the process of painting, to finding the appropriate expression in paint for the everyday objects of his choice. Part, at least, of our enjoyment of his art springs from a recognition of the wonderful process of transformation by which his paint acquires the character of silk or water, silver or glass; and his *Le Bar aux Folies-Bergère* (Plate 121) is one of the most complex examples of this virtuosity. If Manet did not analyse the operation of light with anything like Monet's precision, and if he never achieved in his compositions an informality comparable with that of Degas, he was certainly the founder of the two elements which are characteristic of Impressionism. He introduced the high key in which most of the other Impressionists were to paint, and it was he who first snatched from the passing show those casual moments which are so typical a feature of their art.

Of all the Impressionists, Degas was the one whose artistic education placed him most firmly within the traditions of French art. He studied at the *École des Beaux-Arts*, and then in the studio of Louis Lamothe, a pupil of Ingres. He spent several years in Italy, and his earlier works, however individual they may still appear, were formal portraits and history pieces, all of which show the influence of the *Beaux-Arts* tradition, and the linear methods of Ingres. Already before the Franco-Prussian War of 1870 he had met Manet and other impressionist painters, and he contributed to the first exhibition of the group. A year before that, he had painted a portrait which is not only a turning point in his career but a landmark in nineteenth-century art—the portrait of the Vicomte Lepic with his two daughters. The setting is the *Place de la Concorde*. The Vicomte strides abstractedly out of the right hand edge of the canvas, his cigar thrust between his lips, his umbrella pressed beneath his left arm-pit. His little daughters and their dog loiter around him, and the bottom edge of the canvas cuts off the legs of all three above the knees. The right side of the canvas is filled with an anonymous figure, whose feet and hat-crown are also out of the picture. The empty spaces of the *Place* are animated by a man on horse-back, and the end of a retreating *fiacre*.

This was indeed a new kind of portraiture, the figure being merely snatched for one moment from a casual occurrence; a kind of portrait in which the sitter—how wrong the term seems in reference to a Degas—is not isolated from the common activities of his life.

Degas' means of expression was the human figure, and his main instrument, line (he had said in his youth, "*Je suis né avant tout pour dessiner*"). He was not interested in conventionally beautiful poses, but in the natural movements of men and women as they worked; those particular gestures and actions which belong to their occupations; the strange off-duty attitudes of the ballet dancer as well as the rhythms of the performance (Plate 126), the muscular tensions of a jockey's arms and legs, the angular postures of women bathing, drying their bodies or combing their hair, the stern and powerful movements of a washerwoman (Plate 125). He sought what was vital and characteristic, and for him movement was generally more important than the individual concerned. When, at the end of his life he was too blind to paint, he continued his pursuit in clay.

Degas' art is appropriate to the century in more ways than one. It was in the '70's that the American photographer Muybridge had published those high-speed photographs which showed for the first time the true dynamics of animal movements, and revealed what occurred between those attitudes which were all that earlier artists had been able to record. The movements of Degas' figures reveal those intermediate positions, when the body is poised between one point of balance and another. It is movement in progress, and not movement frozen into an eternal immobility as in a Poussin, where the element of time is rigidly excluded. In a picture by Degas the movement does imply the existence of time, for the forms are passing from one position into another. There is a past and a future as well as a present.

The nineteenth century was profoundly aware of the historical process of time as a sequence of events, and many of its scientific advances emphasised temporal change, just as so much contemporary literature was cast into the form of narrative. The study of geology and the theory of evolution are the most obvious examples of this tendency. In painting, the signs of a similar preoccupation are revealed, and the implication of time is essential to Impressionism. In a Degas it expressed itself through the movements of forms, in a Monet, through the movement of light.

Monet recognised, as Constable had done two generations earlier, that the reality of nature is not something static but something always in motion, moving at the command of light and weather; that a landscape is always in progress passing from one momentary state into another. And his art was devoted to the expression of this reality.

Monet was born in 1840, the son of a grocer, and after working in the company of Boudin and Jongkind, he entered the studio of Gleyre, where Renoir and Sisley were among his fellow students. It was not until he was over forty, had exhibited regularly at the Impressionists' Exhibitions and, in 1870, visited England, where he discovered the art of Turner, that Monet turned from the influences of his early years to the problems which were to absorb him until his death in 1926.

The essence of his experiment was to find in colour a symbol for the play of light over landscape or architecture, through a compromise, indeed, between light and local colour. He pursued this end most logically in several series of paintings: one of haystacks, another of the lily-pond in his garden and a third of the West front of Rouen Cathedral (Plate 128). This shows most obviously how his concentration upon light gradually led to the absence of volume or space, and ultimately to something very near complete abstraction. These paintings also represent the logical conclusion of nineteenth-century naturalism and of that sometimes almost mystical belief in optical experience which is so characteristic of the century.

As to the element of time, it is interesting to notice that in 1909 Monet was tempted to produce a series of pictures, with water-lilies as its theme, which when placed around the walls of a room would give the illusion of "an endless whole, a wave without horizon and without shore".

Alfred Sisley (Plate 130) is close to Monet in his attention to the problems of light, though he never adopted such a consistently analytical approach. He may be said to apply the high key and pure colour of Impressionism to a vision of nature very similar to that of Corot. Camille Pissarro, who was strongly sympathetic to socialism and was the theorist and the thinker of the group, tended to be influenced by the latest movements (he was for a period a follower of Seurat). At the same time, he possessed a sturdier and more traditional vision than Monet.

Of all those who exhibited at the Impressionists' exhibitions it was Renoir who—if we except Cézanne—made the most decisive renunciation of the principles and practices of his colleagues. In 1915 he said to the dealer Ambroise Vollard, referring to a period about 1883, "I had wrung Impressionism dry, and I finally came to the conclusion that I knew neither how to paint nor how to draw. In a word, Impressionism was a blind alley as far as I was concerned." This denial of Impressionism began to show its effect upon Renoir's work after he had paid a visit to Italy in 1880–1, at the age of 40; a visit in which Raphael and Pompeian wall painting were, perhaps, his most important discoveries.

There had been earlier signs, as in *Les Parapluies* (London National Gallery), that his style was moving away from the expression of *Le Moulin de la Galette* (Plate 132), towards a greater clarity and independence of form. Like Monet, Renoir had been born into poverty, and among the work he was forced to undertake during his youth, was painting on china in a Paris porcelain factory. This was as good a preparation as any other for the luminous colouring of Impressionism, and it also gives point to his remark, "Be first of all a good workman; that will not prevent you from having genius."

It was in the '70's that he evolved that particular form of Impressionism which is peculiar to him, and which predicts at least some of the qualities of his later painting. The masterpieces of these years were the *Scènes de la Vie Parisienne*, represented here by Plate 132. These all display a relish for the substance and texture of things, for the spirit of life itself, a delight which brings him closer to Manet than to Monet or to Degas, neither of whom were as much interested in the particular qualities of objects.

In the gaiety and the optimism of these pictures, Renoir went far to recreate the spirit of the eighteenth century, while his delicate fluency of the paint and the attention to texture bring him close to Watteau and Fragonard. In this picture all the people are young, and their mood matches the vivacity of the light which dapples the dark clothes of the men and bright dresses of the girls. This is a Watteau *Fête* without that painter's mysteriousness and indecision.

In the '80's, when this impressionist phase has passed, the tempo slackens, a firm outline regulates the form, and the modelling of the figures becomes as cool and unbroken in its texture as in the paintings of Ingres. This phase, however, lasted only a few years, and by 1890 Renoir was moving towards a monumental art which preserves all that sensuous enjoyment of nature characteristic of his impressionist time.

His last paintings are made of the things which he loved most: the faces of young people, the female nude, fruit and flowers. These paintings, for all their true originality, are strongly reminiscent of Rubens. They have all the richness of form, and enjoyment of the texture in living and growing things which were characteristic of the earlier master. The flesh is vividly warm and set against a cool background, so that the figures, whose sinuous contours combine in a flowing, baroque rhythm, have the fullness of ripe fruit.

\*

IMPRESSIONISM dissatisfied Renoir because it failed to present the things he loved in the full richness of their form and texture. This awareness of the particular limitations of Impressionism was shared by the four artists who stand pre-eminently at the threshold of twentieth-century art: the three Frenchmen, Cézanne, Gauguin and Seurat, and the Dutchman, Van Gogh. Cézanne's, "Monet is only an eye", Gauguin's, "They (the Impressionists) heed only the eye and neglect the mysterious centres of thought", and Van Gogh's assertion that a religious picture cannot be painted in an impressionist manner, are tokens of their discontent. For all of them, however, an impressionist phase was essential to their development. It gave them the freedom of their box of colours and of the world of common experience.

Cézanne came to Paris from his birth-place, Aix-en-Provence, in 1861, when he was twenty-two. During the next fifteen years, mainly under the influence, first of Manet and then of Pissarro, he abandoned an early preference for subject pictures and lightened his palette until it was dominated by those primary and secondary colours which rule his mature painting. His most significant work, however, dates from the last thirty years of his life when he was living most of the time in Provence.

Gauguin also served his apprenticeship under Impressionism. He was the son of a Parisian journalist who had married a Peruvian wife, and he spent his early years in Lima. After being educated at a Jesuit seminary in France until he was seventeen, he spent six years in the merchant marine and ten in the office of an insurance broker. Reasonably prosperous and happily married, he painted as a hobby and had a modest collection of contemporary pictures, including works by Monet. In 1884 he gave up his business career and family life to become a professional painter.

It was not until 1889, however, during the year which he spent at Pont-Aven in Brittany, that he abandoned Impressionism. In such pictures as *The Yellow Christ* or *Jacob's Fight with the Angel* he divided his canvas into planes of flat, unbroken colour. There is no envelope of light or atmosphere in these paintings. Colour is emancipated from the claims of that 'prob-ability' which he found so restrictive in Impressionism. Each form is defined and separated from its neighbour by a firm, organic contour and the pictures lack not only that classical perspective which a painter like Monet had also neglected, but that aerial perspective upon which the impressionist illusion of space was founded. The forms are crowded against the surface of the canvas as in pre-Renaissance painting.

Maurice Denis said of the work of Gauguin and his followers at Pont-Aven, "To the bold innovations of the Impressionists and Divisionists, the newcomers added clumsiness of execution and an almost caricatured simplification of form; and that was Symbolism . . . We substituted the theory of equivalence and symbol for the idea of nature seen through a temperament. We asserted that the emotions or states of mind which any sight whatever provoked, found in the artist's imagination signs and plastic equivalents capable of repro-ducing those emotions or states of mind without having necessarily to furnish a copy of the initial sight."

Gauguin brought back into painting the active expression of ideas and emotions in contrast with the passive optical experience of Impressionism. Two years before he broke the last ties with his former life and went to the Pacific, he was, in these Pont-Aven paintings, expressing his sympathy with the primitive, his distrust of that Greek ideal of form which had conditioned European art for five centuries. "Keep the Persians, the Cambodians and a bit of the Egyptians always in mind", he wrote. "The great error is the Greek, however beautiful it may be." In 1891 Gauguin arrived in Tahiti, where he remained until 1893. After an interlude of two years in France, he returned to the Pacific and died there, in the Marquesas Islands, in 1903, at the age of fifty-two. For him art had just passed through "a long period of aberration caused by physics, chemistry, mechanics and the study of nature". The spontaneous, unsophisticated life and culture of Tahiti, the wild brilliance of its landscape, could be a means of revitalising a tired Western vision. His task was to find symbols by which to synthesise the exotic and primitive expression of such a world, and the methods and sensibilities of the European artist. Among the symbols which he devised were a deliberate angularity of form, a decorative calligraphy unlike anything in European art since the Middle Ages, and a glowing, non-representational colour. "I wanted", he wrote, "to suggest an exuberant and wild nature and a tropical sun which sets on fire everything around it."

But colour could be a symbol for something more than the striking visual experiences which he enjoyed in these islands. This is how he described the painting of the picture entitled *Manao Tupapau* or *The Spirit of the Dead Watches*: "These people are very much afraid of the spirit of the dead . . . I must explain this fright with as little literary means as possible, as one did formerly. So I do this: general harmony, sombre, sad, frightening, sounding to the eye like a death knell, the violet, the dark blue and the orange. I make the linen greenish-yellow, because the linen of these savages is different from ours, because it brings on and suggests the factitious light. The Maori woman never lies down in the dark, and yet I do not want any effect of lamplight, it's common. The yellow which connects the orange, yellow and the brown, completes the musical accord. . . ."

In that passage there is a denial of Courbet's realism, that practice of painting only what the eye can see, to which Manet and other Impressionists subscribed. There is an intuitive understanding of the emotional significance of colour which foreshadows the theories expressed by Kandinsky in 1909 in his book *Über das Geistige in der Kunst*. There is that assertion of the painter's right to order his materials as he desires, which is fundamental to the art of the twentieth century.

Cézanne did not admire Gauguin. If "Monet was only an eye", then Gauguin attended too little to visual experience, was too decorative and primitive a painter. Cézanne was as dependent upon what the eye provided, upon his 'sensations' as he called them, as any Impressionist. But in his maturity Cézanne accepted and attempted to recreate more of the visible world than almost any other artist. He accepted the solid presence of objects, and returned to the problem of structure. He accepted the element of space, not just that general space which divides the foreground of a scene from its background, but the space which lies between its component parts. He sought to express not the accidental, shifting iridescence of nature, but the intrinsic colour of nature in all its intensity. He preferred to paint in an even, consistent light. In his pictures light seems to lie within the heart of things and not to glance from their surface.

It is important to appreciate the 'sensation' which Cézanne received from that Provençal landscape which he painted so often. The clarity of its Mediterranean light gives a sharp exposure of the scene. Structure is not just immediately perceptible, but is, indeed, oppressive in its impact upon the sight. The eye may explore a distant rock as intimately as the hand can investigate a pebble at one's feet. Space, in consequence, is something clearly defined, marked out as categorically as if it were a solid form, and the transparency of the light allows colour to burn with an undiffused brightness.

And so one's immediate experience of a painting by Cézanne is that every inch of its surface is in dynamic operation. There are, so to speak, no pianissimo passages, no places where the eye can relax. The eye is not invited to sink into the surface of the picture or to move about behind the canvas in a world of space, for Cézanne accepts the limits of the painter's two-dimensional ground. The tonal range of colour provides him with the means by which to symbolise structure, and in his pursuit of a pictorial space which will respect the unity of the picture plane, he distorts the pattern of optical perspective. He would tilt the horizontal plane of a retreating road or the hole at the mouth of a jug, he would bend the side of a house or a wall towards the spectator (see Plate 135a). He rejected altogether the ærial perspective of Impressionism.

The *View of L'Estaque* (Plate 136) is an excellent example of his methods, though any black and white reproduction is bound to mislead where pictorial construction is founded upon colour. This landscape is seen from several different viewpoints; the surface of the sea has been tilted, so as to reveal more of its surface than could normally be seen, but this distortion only serves to emphasise the presence of the water and the space which its area defines. In the apt phrase of Lionello Venturi, "We see the distant shore to be near at hand without losing the sensation that it is far away".

The painting (Plate 138), which confronts Cézanne's *Grandes Baigneuses* (Plate 137), displays a similar monumentality; it is equally detached from a current of time, and yet it is immediately clear that this effect has been attained without neglecting, as Cézanne did, the particularities of objects and of everyday life. For this picture is also the record of an occasion, one occasion symbolic of many. The boys who embody such a logical world of form and space, are the representatives of humanity. This picture was the first exhibited work of Georges Seurat, who was then aged twenty-one, and it hung almost disregarded in the *Salon des Artistes Indépendents,* a *Salon* with no jury, established as a rival to the *Salon des Beaux-Arts* in this year of 1884.

During the remaining seven years of his brief life Seurat painted, besides a number of landscapes, seascapes, and harbour pictures, five more of such developed compositions, each of which was a distillation of some common activity—the Sunday afternoon promenade, a fairground, a music-hall, a circus and a group of models resting from their poses. For each of these works Seurat made the most careful preparations—compiling an anthology of drawings and oil sketches of every aspect of his subject, fashioning from them the final picture, which comes to represent all that is most representative of the subject. The results are closer than anything else in French art to the late works of Poussin.

Unfortunately Seurat is more widely recognised as the originator of the technical procedure known as Pointillism—a pseudo-scientific method of giving brilliance to the picture surface by painting with small touches of the primary and secondary colours, and a logical extension of that division of colour which had been practised less systematically by such painters as Monet; though Seurat derived his method from Delacroix rather than from Impressionism.

Seurat was naturally fascinated by every new theory of colour and perspective; but unlike his followers, whose talents were not sufficient to sustain such a rigid and essentially valueless system, pointillism did little to divert Seurat from his genius. Indeed his success recalls Roger Fry's remark that "the artist is generally trying very hard to do something which has nothing to do with what he actually accomplishes; that the fundamental quality of his work seems to come out unconsciously as a by-product of his conscious activity".

# CATALOGUE

## ÉDOUARD MANET
### PARIS, 1832–1882

Frontispiece
Detail from 'Olympia', Plate 122

## SCHOOL OF AVIGNON
### SECOND HALF OF FOURTEENTH CENTURY

I

*Courtly Gathering in the Open Air* ('*Scène de cour d'amour*'). Fresco, 190×165 cm. (74¾×65 in.). Detail reproduced without female figure on left of picture. From the 'House of Queen Jeanne' at Sorgues, near Avignon. Paris, Musées Nationaux.

## UNKNOWN PROVENÇAL MASTER
### ABOUT 1400

2

*Le Bienheureux Pierre de Luxembourg presenting a Donor to the Virgin.* Wood, 54×42 cm. (21¼× 16½ in.). Worcester (Mass.), Art Museum.

## UNKNOWN MASTER
### ABOUT 1430

3

*Vision of Le Bienheureux Pierre de Luxembourg.* Wood, 78×58 cm. (30¾×22⅞ in.). Avignon, Musée Calvet.

## UNKNOWN MASTER
### (PARIS?) ABOUT 1390–1400

4

*The Virgin presenting a Cistercian Monk to the 'Christ de Pitié'.* Right wing of a diptych. Wood, 34×26 cm. (13⅜×10¼ in.). Berlin, Deutsches Museum.

## MASTER OF THE ANNUNCIATION OF AIX
### ABOUT 1443

5

*Still Life.* Upper section of left wing of Annunciation Triptych. Wood, 25×56 cm. (9⅞×22 in.). Amsterdam, Rijksmuseum.

6

*The Annunciation.* Central panel of Triptych. Wood, 155×176 cm. (61×69¼ in.). Altarpiece, probably commissioned about 1443 by Pierre Corpici for his memorial chapel in the Church of Saint-Sauveur at Aix. Dismantled during the 1791 Revolution (see Plates 5–9a). Aix-en-Provence, Sainte-Marie-Madeleine.

7

*Head of Angel.* Detail from Plate 6.

8

*Head of the Virgin.* Detail from Plate 6.

9

*The Prophet Jeremiah.* Wood, 152×86 cm. (59⅞× 33⅞ in.). Right wing of Annunciation Triptych. Brussels, Musée des Beaux-Arts.

9a: Colour Plate

Detail from *The Prophet Jeremiah*, Plate 9.

### UNKNOWN MASTER
#### ABOUT 1475

10

*Saints Anne and Joachim at the Golden Gate.* Fragment; wood, 38×45 cm. (15×17¾ in.). Carpentras, Museum.

### ENGUERRAND DE CHARONTON
#### BORN NEAR LAON, ACTIVE 1444–1464

11

*Coronation of the Virgin.* Wood, 183×220 cm. (72×86⅝ in.). 1453–1454. Commissioned by Jean de Montagnac as altarpiece for the Carthusian Monastery at Villeneuve. Villeneuve-lès-Avignon, Hospice.

12

*Virgin of Mercy.* Detail. About 1452. Wood, total size 66×187 cm. (26×73⅝ in.). Chantilly, Musée Condé.

13

*Madonna.* Detail from Plate 11.

### JEAN FOUQUET
#### TOURS, ABOUT 1415/1420–1477/1481

14

*Portrait of Charles VII of France.* Wood, 86×72 cm. (33⅞×28¾ in.). Probably originally in the Ste-Chapelle at Bourges. Paris, Louvre.

15

*Étienne Chevalier and St. Stephen.* Wood, 93×85 cm. (36⅝×33½ in.). Left half of diptych. Until end of eighteenth century in the Church at Melun. Berlin, Deutsches Museum.

16

*St. Stephen.* Detail from Plate 15.

17

*Étienne Chevalier.* Detail from Plate 15.

18a: Colour Plate

*Madonna with Child and Angels.* Right half of diptych. Until end of eighteenth century in the Church at Melun (see also plates 15–17). Wood, 93×82 cm. (36⅝×32¼ in.). Antwerp, Kgl. Museum.

### SCHOOL OF JEAN FOUQUET
#### ABOUT 1470–1480

18

*Pietà with Donor.* Wood, 147×236 cm. (57⅞×92⅞ in.). Nouans, Parish Church. Now frequently attributed to Fouquet himself.

### NICOLAS FROMENT
#### UZÈS, ABOUT 1435–AVIGNON, 1484

19

Triptych with *Moses and the Burning Bush* on the central panel and *King René and his Wife as Donors* on the wings. Wood, central panel 410×305 cm. (161⅜×120⅛ in.). Commissioned by René of Anjou, King of the two Sicilies, for the High Altar of the Carmelite Church at Aix, and completed in 1476. Aix-en-Provence, Cathedral of Saint-Sauveur.

### LOUIS BRÉA
#### ACTIVE IN LIGURIA AND NICE, 1475–1519

20

Triptych with *Pietà* on the central panel and *Saints Martin and Catherine* on the wings. Wood, central panel 224×130 cm. (88⅛×51⅛ in.). Dated 1475. Nice, Église de Cimiez.

21

*St. Martin.* Detail from left wing of triptych, Plate 20.

## NICOLAS FROMENT
### (see 19)

22

*Moses and the Burning Bush.* Central panel of triptych, Plate 19.

23

*King René of Anjou.* Detail from left wing of triptych, Plate 19.

## MASTER OF MOULINS
### ACTIVE IN BURGUNDY ABOUT 1480–1500

24

*Anne de Beaujeu, Daughter of Louis XI, Duchess of Bourbon.* Detail from right wing of Moulins Triptych (see Plate 25). Moulins, Cathedral.

25

Triptych. Central panel shows *The Virgin and Child in Glory*; wings show *Peter II of Bourbon and his Wife Anne de Beaujeu* (see Plate 24) *as Donors with two Patron Saints.* Wood, 157×283 cm. (61¾×111⅜ in.). About 1498–1499; executed as a commission for Count Peter II of Bourbon. Moulins, Cathedral.

26

*The Nativity with Donor Cardinal Jean Rollin.* Wood, 55×73 cm. (21⅝×28¾ in.). About 1480. Autun, Musée Municipal.

27

*Madonna and Child.* Detail from central panel of Moulins Triptych, Plate 25.

28

*St. Victor and a Donor.* Wood, 56×46 cm. (22×18⅛ in.). Glasgow, Corporation Art Gallery.

## SCHOOL OF AVIGNON
### SECOND HALF OF FIFTEENTH CENTURY

29

*Pietà de Villeneuve.* Wood, 162×218 cm. (63¾× 85⅞ in.). Formerly in the Carthusian Monastery at Villeneuve-lès-Avignon. Paris, Louvre.

30

*Adoration with Mary and a Donor accompanied by his Patron Saint.* About 1500. Wood, 95×110 cm. (37⅜×43¼ in.). Avignon, Musée Calvet.

31

*Donor.* Detail of Plate 30.

32

*St. Jerome.* Second half of fifteenth century. Wood, 54×41 cm. (21¼×16⅛ in.). Paris, Louvre.

## SIMON MARMION
### BORN AT AMIENS, IN LILLE 1454, ACTIVE IN VALENCIENNES 1458–1489

33–34

*Two scenes from the Altar of St. Omer, depicting episodes from the life of St. Bertin.* 1459. Wood, size of single wings 147×56 cm. (57⅞×22 in.). Foundation of Guillaume Filastre, Abbot of St. Bertin in St. Omer, and Bishop of Toul. From the Staatlichen Museen, Berlin (Deutsches Museum).

33

*St. Bertin dividing Water from Wine.* Detail.

34

*Foundation and Construction of the Monastery.*

## FRANÇOIS CLOUET
### TOURS, ABOUT 1522–PARIS, 1572

35

*Portrait of Elisabeth de Valois, daughter of Henry II and later wife of Philip II of Spain.* About 1558–1559. Wood, 36×25 cm. (14⅛×9⅞ in.). Toledo (Ohio), Museum of Arts.

UNKNOWN MASTER
SIXTEENTH CENTURY
35a: Colour Plate
*Portrait of Elisabeth d'Autriche (1554–1592), Queen of France, Daughter of Emperor Maximilian II,– at the age of seventeen.* Wood, 36 × 27 cm. (14⅛ × 10⅝ in.). Paris, Louvre. Painted by an unknown master and, for a long time, erroneously attributed to François Clouet.

FRANÇOIS CLOUET (see 35)
36
*Portrait of the Paris Apothecary and Botanist, Pierre Quthe.* 1552. Wood, 91 × 70 cm. (35⅞ × 27⅝ in.). Paris, Louvre.

37
*Equestrian Portrait of François I.* About 1545. Wood, 27 × 22 cm. (10⅝ × 8⅝ in.). Florence, Uffizi.

38
*Portrait of Charles IX of France.* Dated 1563. Canvas, 222 × 115 cm. (87⅜ × 45¼ in.). Vienna, Kunsthistorisches Museum.

CORNEILLE DE LYON (DE LA HAYE)
BORN IN THE HAGUE, DIED IN LYON (?)
ABOUT 1574
39
*Portrait of a Boy.* Wood, 18 × 15 cm. (7⅛ × 5⅞ in.). Boston, Museum of Fine Arts.

SCHOOL OF FONTAINEBLEAU
40
*The Huntress Diana.* About 1550. Wood, 192 × 133 cm. (75⅝ × 52⅜ in.). Paris, Louvre.

41
*Sabina Poppæa (Wife of Nero).* About 1550–1560. Wood, 82 × 66 cm. (32¼ × 26 in.). Geneva, Musée d'Art et d'Histoire.

42
*Peace.* About 1560–1570. 99 × 75 cm. (39 × 29½ in.). Aix-en-Provence, Museum.

43
*Gabrielle d'Estrées, Mistress of Henry IV, with her Sister, the Duchess of Villars.* About 1594. Wood, 96 × 125 cm. (37¾ × 49¼ in.). Paris, Louvre.

44
*The Reapers.* Canvas, 85 × 112 cm. (33½ × 44⅛ in.). French Master, probably Niccolo dell'Abbate or one of his followers. About 1550–1560. From the Musée de Fontainebleau. Paris, Petit Palais.

45
*The Birth of John the Baptist.* Sixteenth century. Canvas, 94 × 130 cm. (37 × 51⅛ in.). Paris, Louvre.

A. BAUGIN
BORN PROBABLY BETWEEN 1590
AND 1600
46
*Still Life: Allegory of the Five Senses.* Probably painted about 1630. Wood, 55 × 73 cm. (21⅝ × 28¾ in.). Paris, Louvre.

ANTOINE LE NAIN
LAON, ABOUT 1588–PARIS, 1648
47
*Family Group ('Réunion de famille').* 1642. Copper plate, 32 × 40 cm. (12⅝ × 15¾ in.). Paris, Louvre.

LOUIS LE NAIN
LAON, ABOUT 1593–PARIS, 1648
48
*Peasant Family.* Canvas, 113 × 159 cm. (44½ × 62⅝ in.). Paris, Louvre.

### 49

*Return of the Haymakers ('La Charrette').* Canvas, 56×72 cm. (22×28⅜ in.). Dated 1641. Paris, Louvre.

## MATHIEU LE NAIN
### LAON, ABOUT 1607-PARIS, 1677

### 50

*The Dancing Lesson.* Canvas, 95×120 cm. (37⅜× 47¼ in.). About 1655-1660. Paris, Maurice Bérard Collection.

## LOUIS LE NAIN
### (see 48)

### 51

Detail from *Peasant Family*, Plate 48.

### 51a: Colour Plate

Detail from *Peasant Family*, Plate 48.

## GEORGES DE LA TOUR
### VIC-SUR-SEILLE (MOSELLE), 1593-LUNÉVILLE, 1652

### 52

*Adoration of the Shepherds.* Canvas, 107×131 cm. (42⅛×51⅝ in.). Paris, Louvre.

### 53

*St. Jerome in his Study.* Canvas, 123×94 cm. (48⅜×37⅜ in.). Paris, Louvre.

### 54

*St. Irene and her Maidservants lamenting the Death of St. Sebastian.* About 1630-1635. Canvas, 160×129 cm. (63×50¾ in.). Berlin, Kaiser-Friedrich-Museum.

## EUSTACHE LE SUEUR (LESUEUR)
### PARIS, 1617-1655

### 55

*Melpomene, Erato and Polyhymnia.* Wood, 130× 130 cm. (51⅛×51⅛ in.). From the 'Muses' Room' at the Hôtel Nicolas Lambert de Thorigny. About 1645. Paris, Louvre.

## SIMON VOUET
### PARIS, 1590-1649

### 56

*Allegorical figure representing Wealth (also formerly known as 'La Victoire tenant Louis XIII enfant').* Canvas, 170×124 cm. (66⅞×48⅞ in.). Originally in the Palace at Saint-Germain-en-Laye, later at Versailles. Paris, Louvre.

## NICOLAS POUSSIN
### LES ANDELYS (NORMANDIE), 1594-ROME, 1665

### 57

*Summer: Ruth in the Fields of Boaz ('L'Été ou Ruth et Booz').* From the 'Four Seasons'. About 1660-1664. Canvas, 118×160 cm. (46½×63 in.). Paris, Louvre.

### 58

*Autumn: The Spies from Canaan ('L'Automne ou la grappe de la Terre promise').* From the 'Four Seasons'. About 1660-1664. Canvas, 118×160 cm. (46½×63 in.). Paris, Louvre.

### 59

*Bacchanalian Dance.* Canvas, 100×143 cm. (39⅜ ×56¼ in.). London, National Gallery.

### 59a: Colour Plate

*The Kingdom of Flora.* About 1635-1640. Canvas, 131×181 cm. (51⅝×71¼ in.). Dresden, Gemäldegalerie.

60

*Orpheus and Eurydice. Detail.* 1659. Canvas, total size 124×200 cm. (48⅞×78¾ in.). Paris, Louvre.

61

*Rinaldo and Armida.* About 1635. Canvas, 80×106 cm. (31½×41¾ in.). Dulwich, Gallery of Alleyn's College of God's Gift.

## JAQUES BLANCHARD
### PARIS, 1600–1638

62

*Angelica and Médor.* Canvas, 126×186 cm. (49⅝×73¼ in.). New York, Metropolitan Museum.

## SÉBASTIEN BOURDON
### MONTPELLIER, 1616–PARIS, 1671

63

*Self-Portrait.* About 1638. Canvas, 130×97 cm. (51⅛×31⅛ in.). Paris, Louvre.

## PHILIPPE DE CHAMPAIGNE
### BRUSSELS, 1602–PARIS, 1674

64

*Portrait of a Lady* (possibly Madame Le Maître who, after her husband's death in 1634, became Mère Catherine de Saint-Jean of Port-Royal). Canvas, 61×51 cm. (24×20⅛ in.). Paris, Louvre.

## FRANÇOIS PUGET
### DIED 1707

65

*Portrait of his Father, the Sculptor Pierre Puget* (*1620–1694*). Between 1680 and 1690. Canvas, 75×61 cm. (29½×24 in.). Paris, Louvre.

## CLAUDE GELLÉE
### KNOWN AS CLAUDE LORRAIN
### CHAMAGNE, 1600–ROME, 1682

66

*Mercury stealing the Herds of Admetus.* Canvas, 55×45 cm. (21⅝×17¾ in.). About 1647. Rome, Galleria Doria.

67

*Landscape with Christ and the Magdalene.* 1681(?). Canvas, 83×139 cm. (32⅝×54¾ in.). Frankfurt a.M., Städelsches Kunstinstitut.

68

*Harbour in the Fog* ('*Vue d'un port de mer; effet de soleil voilé par une brume*'). 1646. Canvas, 119×150 cm. (46⅞×59 in.). Paris, Louvre.

## CHARLES LE BRUN (LEBRUN)
### PARIS, 1619–1690

69

*Chancellor Séguier.* The occasion is probably the entry of the Infanta Maria Theresa into Paris in 1600. Canvas, 295×350 cm. (116½×137¾ in.). Paris, Louvre.

## NICOLAS DE LARGILLIÈRE
### PARIS, 1656–1746

70

*Self-Portrait with his Wife and Daughter.* Canvas, 149×200 cm. (58⅝×78¾ in.). Paris, Louvre.

## JEAN-BAPTISTE OUDRY
### PARIS, 1686–BEAUVAIS, 1755

71

*Still Life: The White Duck.* Dated 1753. Canvas, 98×64 cm. (38⅝×25¼ in.). London, Sir Philip Sassoon.

## François DESPORTES
### CHAMPIGNEULLES (CHAMPAGNE), 1661–PARIS, 1743

#### 72

*Self-Portrait ('Portrait d'un chasseur').* 1699. Canvas, 197×163 cm. (77⅝×64⅛ in.). Paris, Louvre.

## Nicolas LANCRET
### PARIS, 1690–1743

#### 73

*Summer or The Dance ('L'Été ou la danse').* Canvas, 69×89 cm. (27⅛×35 in.). Paris, Louvre.

## Jean-Antoine WATTEAU
### VALENCIENNES, 1684–NOGENT-SUR-MARNE, 1721

#### 74

*Embarkation for Cytherea ('Fête galante. L'embarquement pour l'île de Cythère').* 1717. Canvas, 129×194 cm. (50¾×76⅜ in.). Paris, Louvre.

#### 75

*'Gilles.'* Canvas, 184×150 cm. (72½×59 in.). Paris, Louvre.

#### 75a: Colour Plate

*'L'Indifférent.'* Wood, 26×20 cm. (10¼×7⅞ in.). Paris, Louvre.

#### 76

*'La Finette.'* Wood, 25×19 cm. (9⅞×7½ in.). Paris, Louvre.

#### 77/78

*Signboard painted for the Art Dealer Gersaint.* Canvas, 163×304 cm. (64⅛×119⅝ in.). Acquired by Frederick the Great before 1756. Charlottenburg (Berlin), Palace.

## François BOUCHER
### PARIS, 1703–1770

#### 79

*Diana Bathing ('Diane sortant du bain').* 1742. Canvas, 57×73 cm. (22½×28¾ in.). Paris, Louvre.

#### 80

*'L'Odalisque.'* Detail. About 1745. Canvas, total size 53×63 cm. (20⅞×24¾ in.). Paris, Louvre.

## Jean-Baptiste-Siméon CHARDIN
### PARIS, 1699–1779

#### 81

*Return from Market ('La Pourvoyeuse').* 1738. Canvas, 46×37 cm. (18⅛×14⅝ in.). Potsdam, Neues Palais.

#### 82

*Boy with Top ('L'enfant au toton').* 1738. Canvas, 38×76 cm. (15×29⅞ in.). Paris, Louvre.

#### 83

*Still Life: Allegory of the Fine Arts.* Canvas, 55×112 cm. (21⅝×44⅛ in.). Executed as a commission for Empress Catherine II of Russia. Leningrad Hermitage.

#### 83a: Colour Plate

*Basket of Peaches on a Stone Table.* Dated 1768. Canvas, 33×40 cm. (13×15¾ in.). Paris, Louvre.

## Charles-André (Carle) VAN LOO
### NICE, 1705–PARIS, 1765

#### 84

*Hunt Breakfast ('Un déjeuner de chasse').* Canvas, 222×250 cm. (87⅜×98⅜ in.). Paris, Louvre.

## Joseph-Siffred DUPLESSIS
### CARPENTRAS, 1725–VERSAILLES, 1808

#### 85

*Portrait of Madame Lenvoir.* Exhibited 1764. Canvas, 63×53 cm. (24¾×20⅞ in.). Paris, Louvre.

JEAN-BAPTISTE PERRONNEAU

PARIS, 1715–AMSTERDAM, 1783

86

*Boy with a Book.* About 1746 (?). Canvas, 63×
62 cm. (24¾×24⅜ in.). Leningrad, Hermitage.

JEAN-HONORÉ FRAGONARD

GRASSE, 1732–PARIS, 1806

87

*The Abbé de Saint-Non in Spanish Costume.* About
1769. Canvas, 100×74 cm. (39⅜×29⅛ in.).
Paris, Paul Cailleux Collection.

88

*The Billet-Doux.* Canvas, 80×64 cm. (31½×25¼
in.). New York, J. S. Bache Collection.

89

*The Storm* ('*L'Orage*'). Canvas, 97×73 cm.
(38⅛×28¾ in.). Paris, Louvre.

90

'*Gimblette.*' Canvas. Private Collection.

HUBERT ROBERT

PARIS, 1744–1808

91

*Pont du Gard.* 1787. Canvas, 242×242 cm.
(95¼×95¼ in.). Paris, Louvre.

JAQUES-LOUIS DAVID

PARIS, 1748–BRUSSELS, 1825

92

'*Marat Assassiné.*' 1793. Canvas, 165×128 cm.
(65×50⅜ in.). Brussels, Musée des Beaux-Arts.

93

*The Oath of the Horatii* ('*Le serment des Horaces
entre les mains de leur père*'). 1784. Canvas, 330×
427 cm. (129⅞×168⅛ in.). Paris, Louvre.

94

*Madame Récamier.* 1800. Canvas, 173×243 cm.
(68⅛×95⅝ in.). Paris, Louvre.

95

*Madame Chalgrin* (?). 1793(?). Detail. Canvas,
total size 130×98 cm. (51⅛×38⅝ in.). Paris,
Louvre.

JEAN-ANTOINE GROS

PARIS, 1771–BAS-MEUDON, 1835

96

*Portrait of Lieutenant Legrand.* 1810. Canvas,
250×175 cm. (98⅜×68⅞ in.). Paris, Duc de
Trévise Collection.

97

*The Plague of Jaffa* ('*Les pestiférés de Jaffa*').
Canvas, 532×720 cm. (209½×283⅛ in.). Paris,
Louvre.

THÉODORE GÉRICAULT

ROUEN, 1791–PARIS, 1824

98

*The Raft of the Medusa* ('*Le radeau de la Méduse*').
Exhibited 1819. Canvas, 38×46 cm. (15×18⅛
in.). Paris, Louvre.

99

*Madman* ('*Le fou assassin*' ou '*La monomanie du vol*').
From a series of ten studies of mental patients
which Géricault painted for his friend Dr.
Georget, between 1821 and 1824. Canvas, 61×
51 cm. (24×20⅛ in.). Ghent, Musée des Beaux-
Arts.

99a: Colour Plate

*Mad Woman* ('*La folle*' ou '*La monomanie du jeu*').
Detail. From the same series as 99 above. Canvas,
total size 77×64 cm. (30¼×25¼ in.). Paris,
Louvre.

## FRANÇOIS-PASCAL-SIMON GÉRARD
### ROME, 1770–PARIS, 1837

#### 100
*Mademoiselle Zoé Jacqueline du Vidal de Montferrier.* Canvas, Marquis de Montferrier Collection.


## JEAN-DOMINIQUE-AUGUSTE INGRES
### MONTAUBAN, 1780–PARIS, 1867

#### 101
*Portrait of Louis-François Bertin aîné.* 1832. Canvas, 116×95 cm. (45⅝×37⅜ in.). Paris, Louvre.

#### 102
*Mademoiselle Rivière.* 1805. Canvas, 100×70 cm. (39⅜×27⅝ in.). Paris, Louvre.

#### 103
'*La Grande Odalisque.*' Canvas, 91×162 cm. (35⅞ ×63¾ in.). Commissioned by Queen Caroline of Naples and executed in Rome, 1814. Paris, Louvre.


## EUGÈNE DELACROIX
### CHARENTON, 1798–PARIS, 1863

#### 104
*Asters and Balsamines.* About 1850. Canvas, 74× 93·5 cm. (29⅛×36¾ in.). Zurich, Kunsthaus.

#### 105
*Self-Portrait.* About 1835–1839. Canvas, 65×55 cm. (25⅝×21⅝ in.). Paris, Louvre.

#### 106
*The Massacre of Scio* ('*Scènes des massacres de Scio*'). Acquired by Charles X from the Salon of 1824. Canvas, 422×357 cm. (166⅛×140⅛ in.). Paris, Louvre.

#### 107
*The twenty-eighth of July* ('*Le 28 juillet 1830: La liberté guidant le peuple*'). Acquired by Louis-Philippe from the Salon of 1831. Canvas, 260×325 cm. (102⅜×128 in.). Paris, Louvre.

#### 107a: Colour Plate
*Still Life with Lobsters.* Painted at Beffes for General de Coëtlosquet. Canvas, 80×100 cm. (31½×39⅜ in.). Paris, Louvre.

#### 108
*Tobias and the Angel.* 1863. Canvas, 40·5×32·5 cm. (16×12⅞ in.). Winterthur, Oskar Reinhart Collection.


## THÉODORE CHASSÉRIAU
### LE LIMON À SAINTE-BARBE DE SAMANA (SAN DOMINGO), 1819–PARIS, 1856

#### 109
*The Artist's two Sisters.* 1843. Canvas, 180×135 cm. (70⅞×53⅛ in.). Paris, Louvre.


## JEAN-FRANÇOIS MILLET
### GRUCHY (MANCHE), 1814–BARBIZON, 1875

#### 110
*Portrait of a Naval Officer.* 1845. Canvas, 79×63 cm. (31⅛×24¾ in.). Lyon, Palais des Beaux-Arts.


## HONORÉ DAUMIER
### MARSEILLE, 1808–VALMONDOIS, 1879

#### 111
*The Drama: Audience watching 'Hamlet'.* Canvas, 98×90 cm. (38⅝×35⅜ in.). Munich, Neue Staatsgalerie.

#### 112
*The Washerwoman* ('*La Blanchisseuse*'). About 1861–1863. Wood, 49×33 cm. (19¼×13 in.). Paris, Louvre.

## Jean-baptiste-camille COROT
### PARIS, 1796–1875

#### 113
*Breton Woman feeding her Child.* Copper plate, 33×25 cm. (13×9⅞ in.). Winterthur, Oskar Reinhart Collection.

#### 114
*'La Femme à la Perle.'* 1868–1870. Canvas, 70×54 cm. (27⅝×21¼ in.). Paris, Louvre.

#### 115
*Chartres Cathedral.* 1830. Canvas, 65×50 cm. (25⅝×19⅝ in.). Paris, Louvre.

#### 115a: Colour Plate
*The Belltower of Douai ('Le beffroi de Douai').* May 1871. Canvas, 46×39 cm. (18⅛×15⅜ in.). Paris, Louvre.

#### 116
*The Bridge at Mantes.* About 1868–1870. Canvas, 38×56 cm. (15×22 in.). Paris, Louvre.

## Gustave COURBET
### ORNANS, 1819–LA TOUR-DE-PEILZ (SWITZERLAND), 1877

#### 117
*Stormy Sea ('Mer orageuse').* 1869. Canvas, 117× 160 cm. (46⅛×63 in.). Paris, Louvre.

#### 118
*Young Girls on the banks of the Seine ('Les demoiselles au bord de la Seine').* 1856. Canvas, 173×206 cm. (68⅛×81⅛ in.). Musée de la ville de Paris (Petit Palais).

## Édouard MANET
### PARIS, 1832–1883

#### 119
*'Le Déjeuner sur l'Herbe.'* 1863. Canvas, 214×270 cm. (84¼×106¼ in.). Paris, Louvre.

#### 120
*At the Breakfast Table.* 1868–1869. Canvas, 120×153 cm. (47¼×60¼ in.). Munich, Neue Staatsgalerie.

#### 121
*'Le Bar aux Folies-Bergère.'* 1881/1882. Canvas, 96×130 cm. (37¾×51⅛ in.). London, Tate Gallery.

#### 122
*'Olympia.'* Painted 1863, exhibited at the Salon 1865, acquired for the National Collections by public subscription in 1890. Canvas, 130×190 cm. (51⅛×74¾ in.). Paris, Louvre.

#### 123
*Argenteuil.* 1874. Canvas, 149×131 cm. (58⅝× 51⅝ in.). Tournai, Museum.

#### 124
*Still Life.* 1865–1867. Canvas, 43×71 cm. (16⅞×28 in.). Paris, Louvre.

## Edgar DEGAS
### PARIS, 1834–1917

#### 125
*Women Ironing ('Les Repasseuses').* 1882. Canvas, 76×82 cm. (29⅞×32¼ in.). Paris, Louvre.

#### 126
*The Dancing Class ('La classe de danse').* 1874. Canvas, 85×75 cm. (33½×29½ in.). Paris, Louvre.

## Camille PISSARO
### SAINT-THOMAS (WEST INDIES), 1831– PARIS, 1903

#### 127
*Rue de l'Épicerie at Rouen.* Canvas.

## CLAUDE MONET
### PARIS, 1840–GIVERNY, 1926

#### 128
*Rouen Cathedral.* 1894. Canvas, 100×65 cm. (39⅜×25⅝ in.). Paris, Louvre.

#### 129
*Gare Saint-Lazare.* Canvas, 98×75 cm. (38⅝× 29½ in.). Paris, Louvre.

## ALFRED SISLEY
### PARIS, 1839–MORET-SUR-LOING, 1899

#### 130
*'La Route, vue de chemin de Sèvres.'* 1873. Canvas, 56×76 cm. (22×29⅞ in.). Paris, Louvre.

## PIERRE-AUGUSTE RENOIR
### LIMOGES, 1841–CAGNES, 1919

#### 131
*Chalands sur la Seine.* About 1869. Canvas, 46× 64 cm. (18⅛×25¼ in.). Paris, Louvre.

#### 132
*'Le Moulin de la Galette.'* 1876. Canvas, 177× 132 cm. (69⅝×52 in.). Paris, Louvre.

#### 133
*Bather.* Canvas, 56×46 cm. (22×18⅛ in.). Winterthur, Georg Reinhart Collection.

## PAUL GAUGUIN
### PARIS, 1848–DOMINIQUE, 1903

#### 134
*Two Tahitian Women ('Femmes au Mango').* 1899. Canvas, 36×28 cm. (14⅛×11 in.). New York, William Church Osborn Collection.

## PAUL CÉZANNE
### AIX-EN-PROVENCE, 1839–1906

#### 135
*Card Players ('Les Joueurs de cartes').* Canvas, 57×47 cm. (22½×18½ in.). Paris, Louvre.

#### 135a: Colour Plate
*Landscape.* Canvas, 65×55 cm. (25⅝×21⅝ in.). Private Collection (Gaston Bernheim de Villers).

#### 136
*View of L'Estaque.* 1883–1885. Canvas, 58×72 cm. (22⅞×28⅜ in.). Paris, Louvre.

#### 137
*The Bathers ('Grandes Baigneuses').* Between 1879– 1882. Canvas, 55×52 cm. (21⅝×20½ in.). Musée de la Ville de Paris (Petit Palais).

## GEORGES-PIERRE SEURAT
### PARIS, 1859–1891

#### 138
*'Une Baignade–Asnières.'* 1883–1884. Canvas, 200 ×301 cm. (78¾×118½ in.). London, Tate Gallery.

## HENRI DE TOULOUSE-LAUTREC
### ALBI, 1864–MALROMÉ, 1901

#### 139
*The Clown Cha-U-Kao at the Moulin Rouge.* 1895. Canvas, 75×55 cm. (29½×21⅝ in.). Winterthur, Oskar Reinhart Collection.

### ACKNOWLEDGMENTS

Alinari, Florence: 94. Walter Dräyer, Zurich: 118. Giraudon, Paris: 5, 12, 18, 26, 37, 39, 86, 88, 92, 100, 126, 134. Linck, Winterthur: 108, 113, 133. Metropolitan Museum, New York: 62. National Gallery, London: 59, 61. Formerly Staatliche Museen, Berlin: 77/78. Städelsches Kunstinstitut, Frankfurt a.M.: 67. Tate Gallery, London: 121, 138. Pinakothek, Munich: 111, 120.

Reproductions of paintings by Degas, Pissarro, Monet, Sisley, Renoir, Gauguin, Seurat (Plates 125–139) appear by courtesy of the Syndicat de la Propriété Artistique (Reproduction réservée S.P.A. 12, Rue Henner, Paris 9e); Plate 139 appears by courtesy of the Musée d'Albi, Albi.

ÉCOLE D'AVIGNON, XIVᵉ SIÈCLE.

2. ANONYME, VERS 1400

3. ANONYME, VERS 1430

4. ANONYME, VERS 1390-1400

5

6. MAITRE DE L'ANNONCIATION D'AIX

7. MAITRE DE L'ANNONCIATION D'AIX

8. MAITRE DE L'ANNONCIATION D'AIX

9. MAITRE DE L'ANNONCIATION D'AIX

10. ANONYME, VERS 1475

11. ENGUERRAND CHARONTON

12. ENGUERRAND CHARONTON

13. ENGUERRAND CHARONTON

14. JEAN FOUQUET

15. JEAN FOUQUET

16. JEAN FOUQUET

17. JEAN FOUQUET

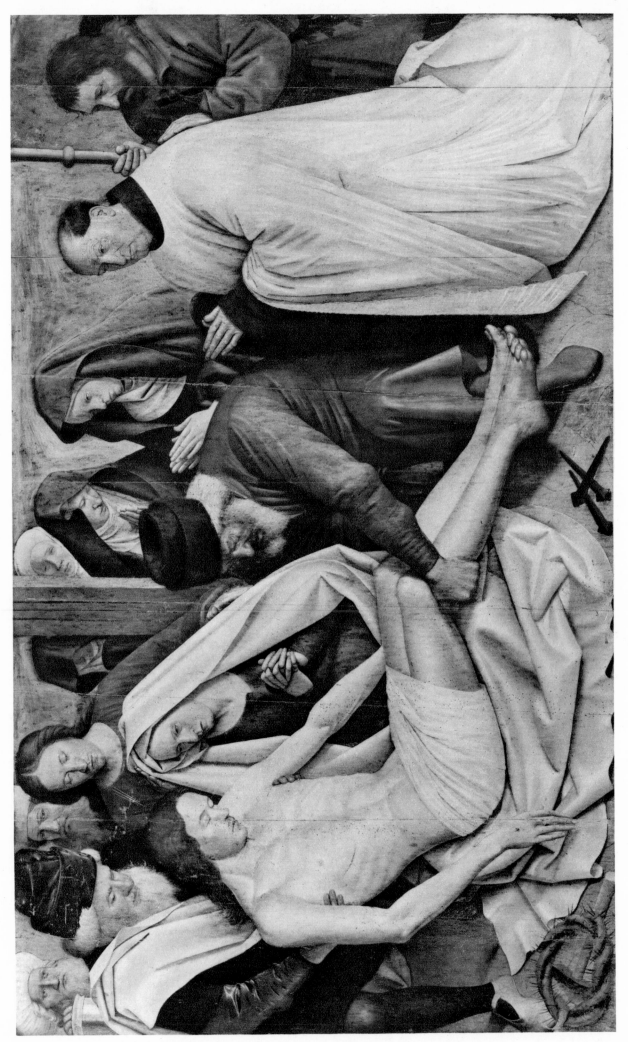

18. ÉCOLE DE JEAN FOUQUET

FOUQUET

19. NICOLAS FROMENT

20. LOUIS BRÉA

21. LOUIS BRÉA

VBVM·QVEM·VIDERAT·MOYSES·INCOMBVSTVM·CONSERVATAM·AGNOVIMVS·TVAM·LAVDABILEM·VIRGINITATEM·SCTA·DEI·GENITRIX

22. NICOLAS FROMENT

23. NICOLAS FROMENT

24. MAITRE DE MOULINS

26. MAITRE DE MOULINS

27. MAITRE DE MOULINS

28. MAITRE DE MOULINS

31. ÉCOLE D'AVIGNON

32. ÉCOLE D'AVIGNON

33. SIMON MARMION

34. SIMON MARMION

35. FRANÇOIS CLOUET

ÉCOLE FRANÇAISE, XVIᵉ SIÈCLE

36. FRANÇOIS CLOUET

37. FRANÇOIS CLOUET

38. FRANÇOIS CLOUET

39. CORNEILLE DE LYON

40. ÉCOLE DE FONTAINEBLEAU

41. ÉCOLE DE FONTAINEBLEAU

42. ÉCOLE DE FONTAINEBLEAU

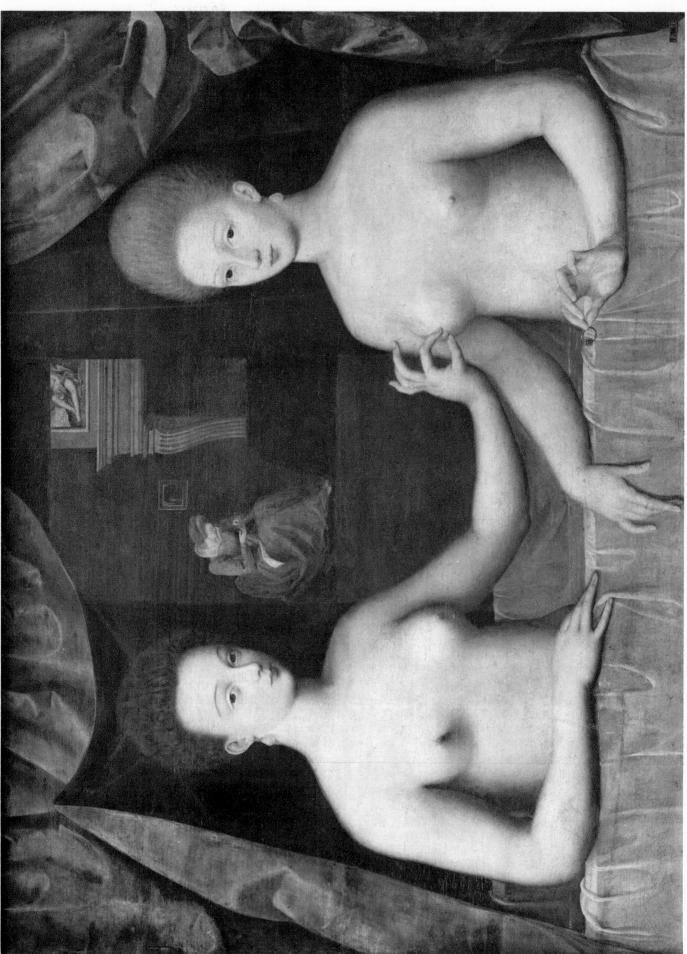

44. ÉCOLE DE FONTAINEBLEAU (NICCOLO DELL'ABBATE)

45. ÉCOLE DE FONTAINEBLEAU

46. A. BAUGIN

48. LOUIS LE NAIN

LOUIS LE NAIN

50. MATHIEU LE NAIN

51. LOUIS LE NAIN

52. GEORGES DE LA TOUR

53. GEORGES DE LA TOUR

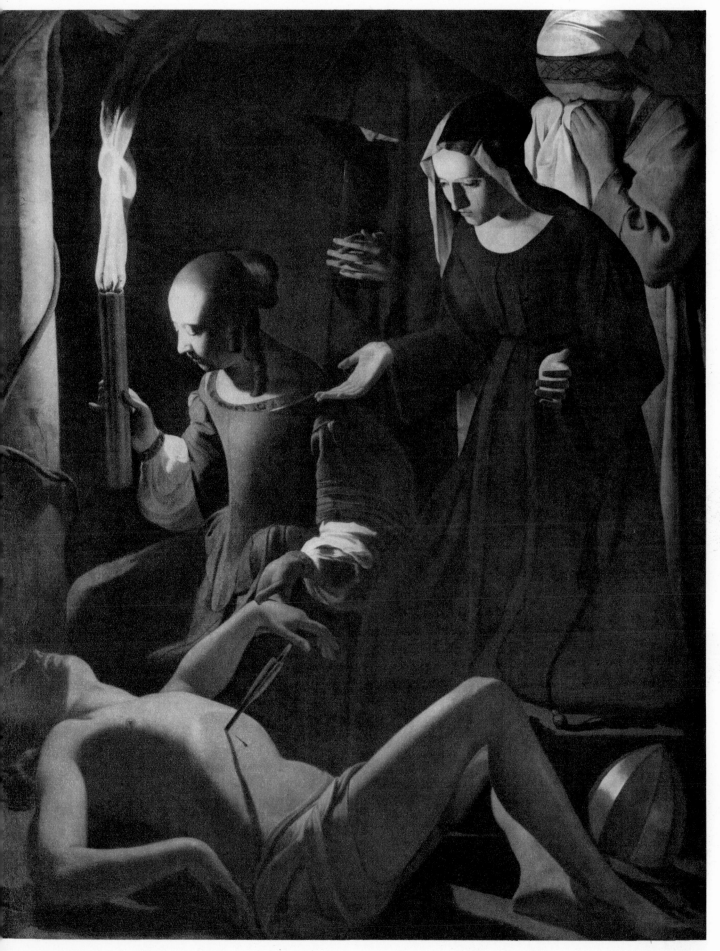

54. GEORGES DE LA TOUR

55. EUSTACHE LE SUEUR

56. SIMON VOUET

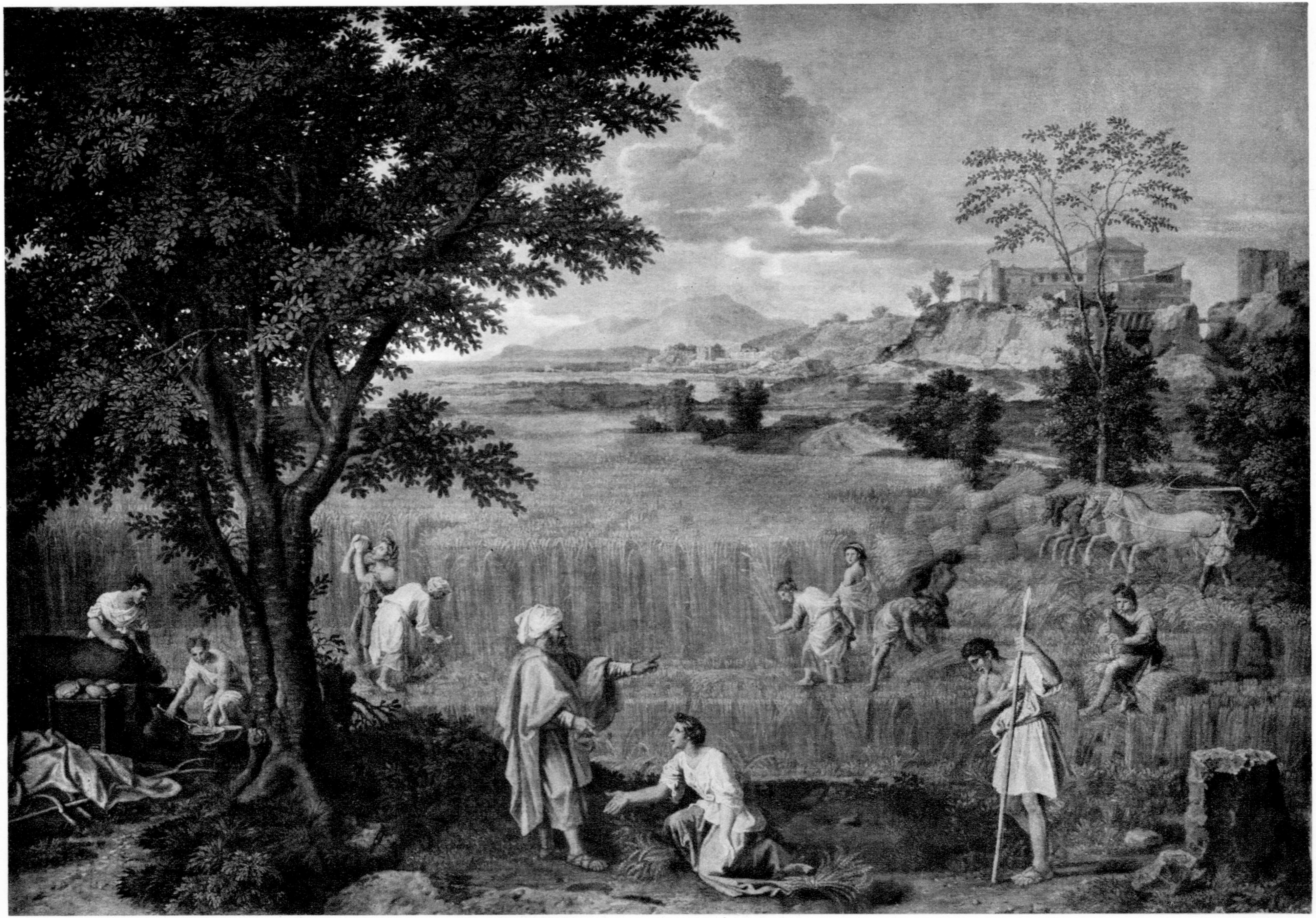

57. NICOLAS POUSSIN

58. NICOLAS POUSSIN

59. NICOLAS POUSSIN

NICOLAS POUSSIN

60. NICOLAS POUSSIN

61. NICOLAS POUSSIN

62. JACQUES BLANCHARD

63. SÉBASTIEN BOURDON

64. PHILIPPE DE CHAMPAIGNE

65. FRANÇOIS PUGET

66. CLAUDE GELLÉE (LE LORRAIN)

67. CLAUDE GELLÉE (LE LORRAIN)

68. CLAUDE GELLÉE (LE LORRAIN)

69. CHARLES LE BRUN

70. NICOLAS DE LARGILLIÈRE

71. JEAN-BAPTISTE OUDRY

72. FRANÇOIS DESPORTES

73. NICOLAS LANCRET

74. ANTOINE WATTEAU

75. ANTOINE WATTEAU

ANTOINE WATTEAU

76. ANTOINE WATTEAU

77./78. ANTOINE WATTEAU

79. FRANÇOIS BOUCHER

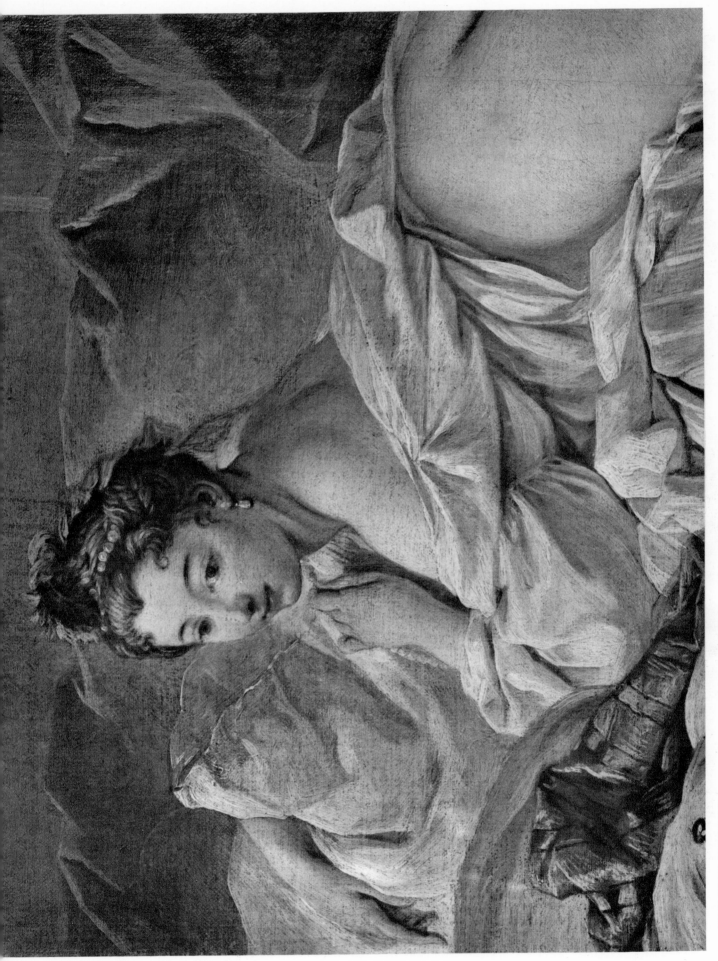

80. FRANÇOIS BOUCHER

81. JEAN-BAPTISTE-SIMÉON CHARDIN

2. JEAN-BAPTISTE-SIMÉON CHARDIN

83. JEAN-BAPTISTE-SIMÉON CHARDIN

JEAN-BAPTISTE-SIMÉON CHARDIN

84. CHARLES-ANDRÉ (CARLE) VAN LOO

85. JOSEPH-SIFFRED DUPLESSIS

86. JEAN-BAPTISTE·PERRONNEAU

87. HONORÉ FRAGONARD

88. HONORÉ FRAGONARD

89. HONORÉ FRAGONARD

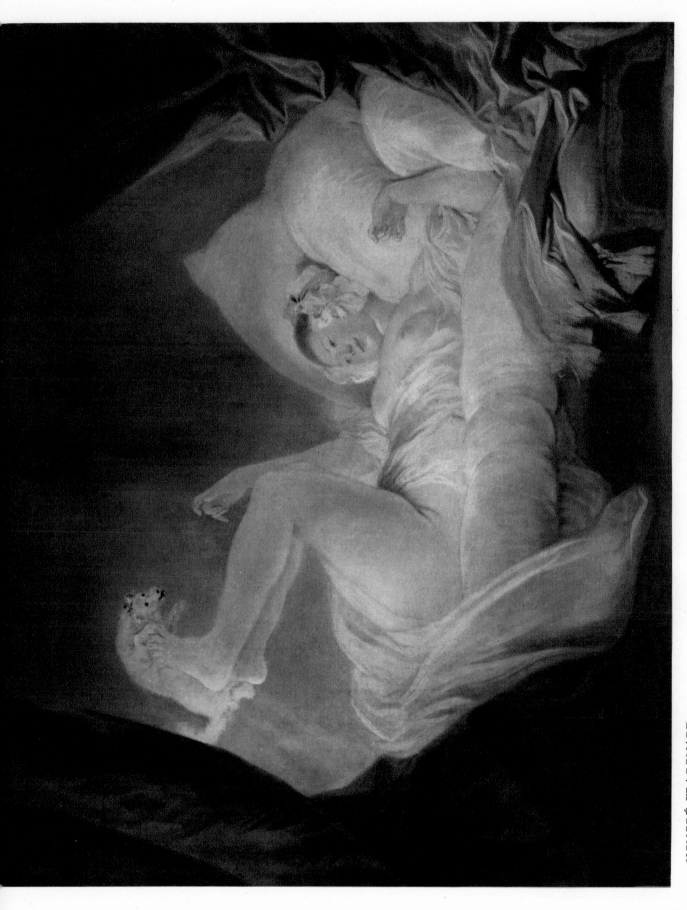

90. HONORÉ FRAGONARD

91. HUBERT ROBERT

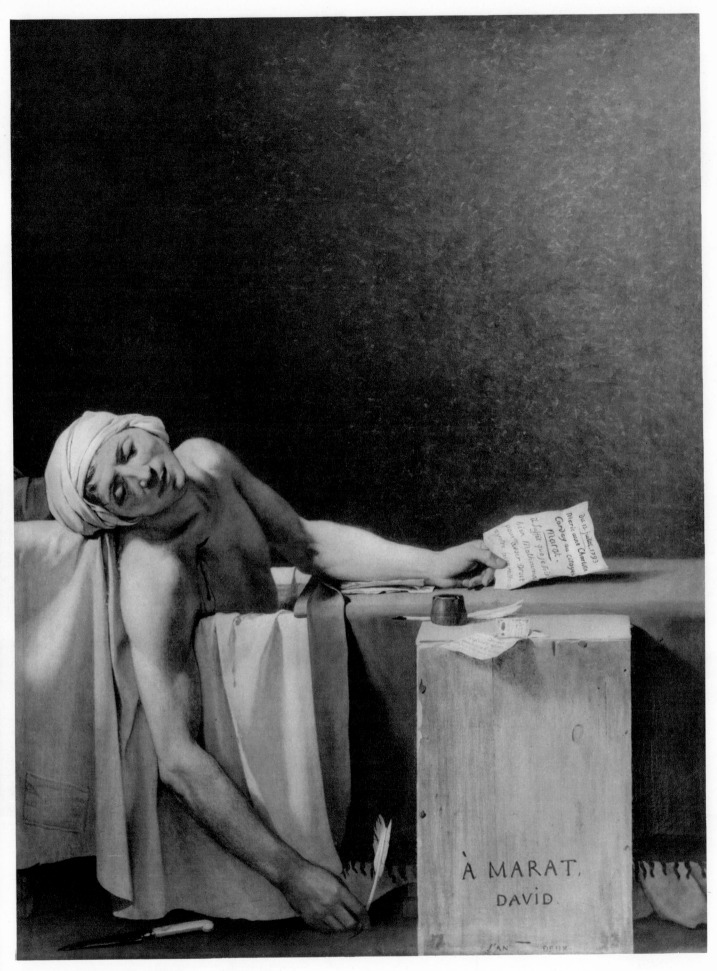

92. JACQUES-LOUIS DAVID

93. JACQUES-LOUIS DAVID

94. JACQUES-LOUIS DAVID

95. JACQUES-LOUIS DAVID

96. JEAN-ANTOINE GROS

98. THÉODORE GÉRICAULT

99. THÉODORE GÉRICAULT

100. FRANÇOIS GÉRARD

101. DOMINIQUE INGRES

102. DOMINIQUE INGRES

103. DOMINIQUE INGRES

105. EUGÈNE DELACROIX

6. EUGÈNE DELACROIX

EUGÈNE DELACROIX

108. EUGÈNE DELACROIX

109. THÉODORE CHASSÉRIAU

110. JEAN-FRANÇOIS MILLET

111. HONORÉ DAUMIER

112. HONORÉ DAUMIER

113. CAMILLE COROT

114. CAMILLE COROT

115. CAMILLE COROT

CAMILLE COROT

116. CAMILLE COROT

117. GUSTAVE COURBET

118. GUSTAVE COURBET

119. EDOUARD MANET

120. EDOUARD MANET

121. EDOUARD MANET

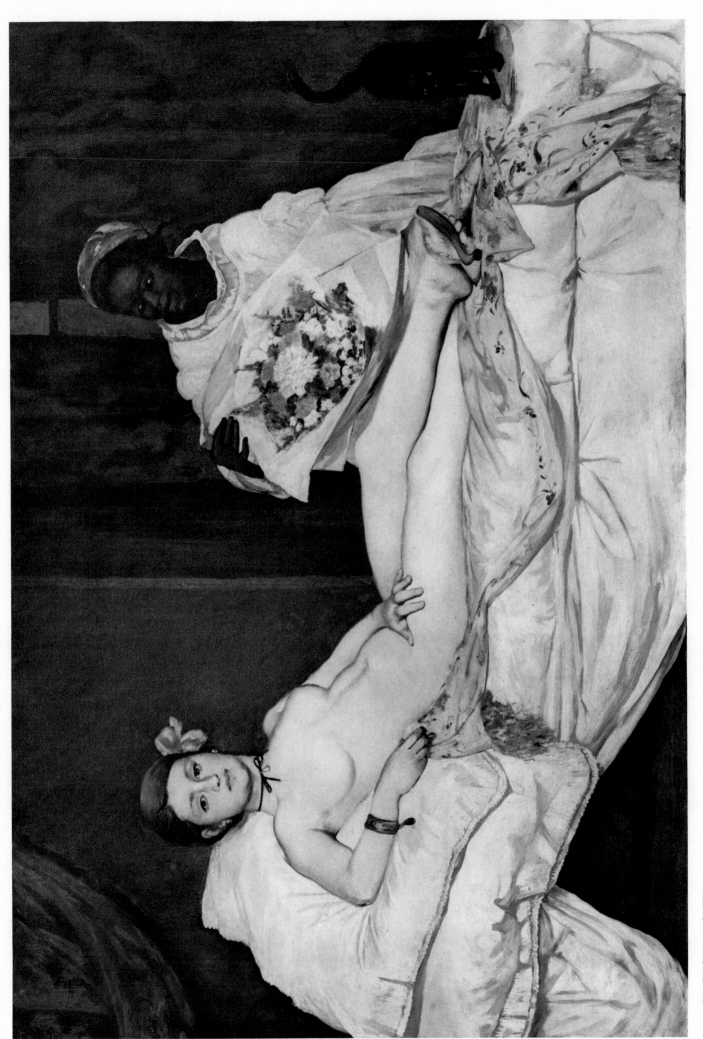

122. EDOUARD MANET

123. EDOUARD MANET

124. EDOUARD MANET

125. EDGAR DEGAS

126. EDGAR DEGAS

127. CAMILLE PISSARRO

128. CLAUDE MONET

129. CLAUDE MONET

130. ALFRED SISLEY

131. AUGUSTE RENOIR

132. AUGUSTE RENOIR

133. AUGUSTE RENOIR

134. PAUL GAUGUIN

135. PAUL CÉZANNE

PAUL CÉZANNE

136. PAUL CÉZANNE

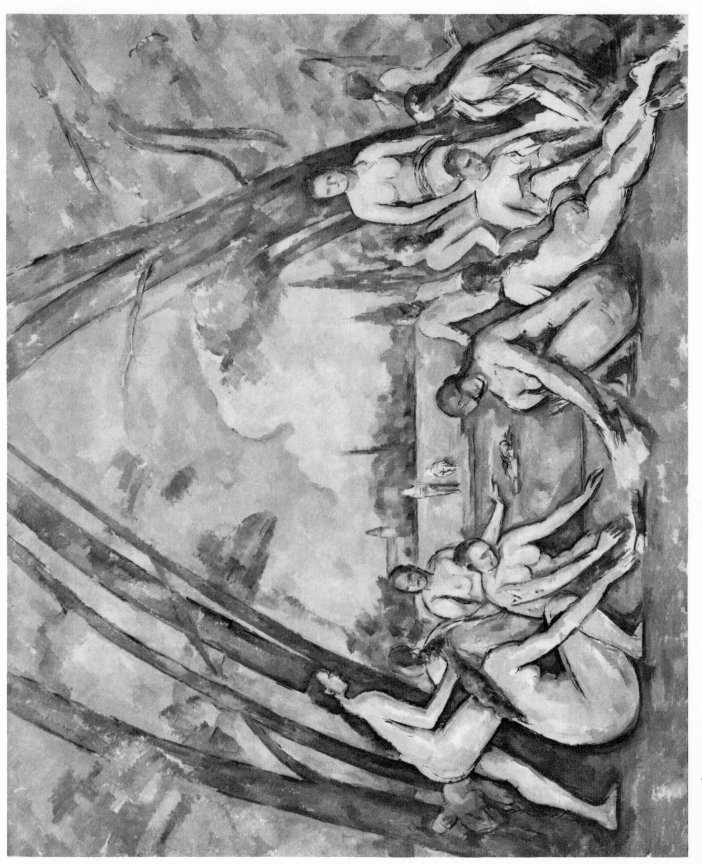

137. PAUL CÉZANNE

138. GEORGES-PIERRE SEURAT

139. HENRI DE TOULOUSE-LAUTREC